# NEW-COVENANT
## VOLUME FOURTEEN

Books by David H.J.Gay referred to in this volume:

*A Case of Mistaken Identity: A Critique of Timothy Keller on Regeneration.*

*Baptist Sacramentalism: A Warning to Baptists.*

*Battle for the Church: 1517-1644 (second edition).*

*Christ Is All: No Sanctification by the Law.*

*Conversion Ruined: The New Perspective and the Conversion of Sinners.*

*Evangelicals Warned: Isaiah 30 Speaks Today.*

*False Brothers: Paul and Today.*

*Four 'Antinomians' Tried and Vindicated: Tobias Crisp, William Dell, John Eaton and John Saltmarsh.*

*Infant Baptism Tested.*

*John Bunyan: Antinomian, New-Covenant Theologian, or...?*

*Justification: The Make-or-Break Doctrine.*

*Luther on Baptism: Sacramentalism in the Raw.*

*New-Covenant Articles Volume One.*

*New-Covenant Articles Volume Two.*

*New-Covenant Articles Volume Four.*

*New-Covenant Articles Volume Eleven.*

*New-Covenant Articles Volume Thirteen.*

*No Safety Before Saving Faith.*

*Priesthood: Our Need, God's Provision.*

*Public Worship: God-Ordained or Man-Invented?*

*Public Worship: God-Ordained or Man-Invented?; Public Worship Notes.*

*Redemption History Through Covenants.*

*Relationship Evangelism Exposed: A Blight on the Churches and the Ungodly.*

*Romans 11: A Suggested Exegesis.*

*Sanctification in Galatians.*

*Spurgeon on the New Covenant.*

*The Hinge in Romans 1 – 8: A critique of N.T.Wright's view of Baptism and Conversion.*

*The Pastor: Does He Exist?*

*The Priesthood of All Believers: Slogan or Substance?*

*The Secret Stifler: Incipient Sandemanianism and Preaching the Gospel to Sinners.*

*Three Verses Misunderstood: Galatians 3:23-25 Expounded.*

*Undervalued Themes: Resurrection and Kingdom.*

# New-Covenant Articles

## *Volume Fourteen*

The covenant of which [Jesus] is mediator is superior to the old one, and it is founded on better promises... By calling this covenant 'new', he has made the first one obsolete

Hebrews 8:6,13

**David H.J.Gay**

**BRACHUS**

BRACHUS 2023
davidhjgay@googlemail.com

Scripture quotations come from a variety of versions

# Contents

Note to the Reader.................................................... 9

New-Covenant Theology: A Summary...................... 11

Three *Ekklēsia* Consequences of Augustine ........... 13

Begg on Baptism: Playing with Fire ....................... 19

Believers One and All .............................................. 25

Paul's Breathtaking Assertion................................. 29

Census Shock! ......................................................... 41

Evangelical Christendom Confusion....................... 51

The Law of Diminishing Returns............................. 55

Flogging a Dead Horse............................................ 59

Salvation in Hebrews .............................................. 63

Ignored Intelligence: The Cost............................... 77

The Case of the Curious Blind Spot........................ 85

Preacher: Postman or Pleader?............................... 95

Touching the Untouchable ...................................... 99

The Question Which Cannot Be Ducked ............... 113

A Disaster Averted: Romans 14:5-6 ..................... 123

Christmas and Romans 14:5-6 .............................. 141

Purim and Christmas.............................................. 147

Reformed Infant Baptismal Regeneration............. 159

Two Phrases to be Reckoned With ........................ 169

National Anthem Verses ........................................ 175

A Tale of Two Coronations: Farcical & Real ....... 177

An Appeal to the Reformed ................................... 187

# Note to the Reader

This is the fourteenth – and final – volume in the series of my collected articles on the new covenant. Although such pieces have been posted on my sermonaudio.com page, once again I not only want to set my work in a more permanent form for those who have already discovered it, but in the hope of reaching a new audience. The fact is, there is a growing body of believers who, having had more than enough of the bondage and fear produced by the law teachers and their clever tricks with Scripture, are displaying a voracious appetite for the liberating gospel of our Lord Jesus Christ. I am thinking of them. If they find any value in these articles, they might like to explore my full-length books.

I express my continued gratitude to Ace and Peggy Staggs for all the internet work they do behind the scenes. I also record my debt to those believers who support me in prayer. Mere words inadequately express what I feel about my brothers and sisters who encourage me in all these ways and more. God will remember them and their labour (Heb. 6:10).

# New-Covenant Theology:
## A Summary

This summary represents my understanding of new-covenant theology. Scriptural justification for these statements may be found throughout my works.

New-covenant theology takes full account of the progressive nature of revelation, and thus it sees the new covenant as the goal and climax of the previous biblical covenants. The Bible is not flat but is progressive in revelation; 'but now' is a critical scriptural phrase marking the disjoint between the old and new covenants. The Old Testament (old covenant) must be interpreted in light of the New (new), not the other way about.

God has one eternal plan centred in Jesus Christ.

The law of Moses was one. It cannot, must not, be divided into three bits. God gave Israel the old covenant as a temporary measure, as a shadow of the person and work of Christ who fulfilled it and rendered it obsolete.

Believers are not under the law of Moses, but under the law of Christ. Having died to the Mosaic law, they are not under that condemning letter, but, by the Spirit, they are in union with Christ, married to him, and thus are enabled, empowered and motivated to live to his glory in obedience to Scripture.

Christ is all. He is his law. He is the covenant.

Believers use the law of Moses as a paradigm (pattern or typical example),[1] as part of 'all Scripture', but not as a list of detailed rules.

Sinners do not have to be prepared for Christ by first being taken to the law.

---

[1] See, for instance, 1 Cor. 5:6-13; 9:8-14; 10:1-11,18; 14:21; 2 Cor. 6:14 – 7:1; 8:15; 13:1.

There is one body of the redeemed, the eschatological Israel, 'the Israel of God' (Gal. 6:16), comprising the redeemed from the time of Adam to Pentecost, and redeemed Jews and Gentiles from that time until the end of the age.

The word 'active' plays a major role in new-covenant theology, and in two respects. *First*, while the redemption of the elect is accomplished through the passive obedience of Christ – that is, through his death on the cross – it is Christ's active obedience – that is, his life-long obedience to his Father in fulfilling the Mosaic law – which is imputed as righteousness to the believer.[2] The believer's justification – that is, his righteousness in Christ by faith alone – is this fulfilment of the law, and not merely pardon from sin. *Secondly*, the believer is enabled by the Spirit to be active – and not passive – in his progressive sanctification; that is, in his obedience by faith to the law of Christ, and proceeding from his faith in Christ.

---

[2] Although I have serious reservations about the words 'active' and 'passive' in this regard, I let the common usage stand.

# *Three* Ekklēsia *Consequences of Augustine*[1]

Augustine of Hippo (354-430), through his prolific works, continues to exercise an influence on Christendom that's hard to overstate. While countless volumes have been written about him and his works,[2] without any hint of patronisation, I want, in a straightforward, non-academic way, to speak to those evangelicals who know little about him, who have never thought about him; I want to draw their attention to three consequences – far-reaching consequences – of Augustine to the life of the *ekklēsia*, consequences which none of us in Christendom can avoid. Originally, I had wanted to use the title 'The *Ekklēsia* Consequences...', but, in order to keep this article in bounds, I have limited these consequences to three. But what a three!

There is a spectrum of views about Augustine. Many, regarding him as the theologian *par excellence*, and, adopting his views, have published their own works developing his doctrines. Roman Catholicism depends heavily on Augustine. But so does the Reformed part of Christendom – Martin Luther was an Augustinian friar, and John Calvin was forever quoting Augustine.

Others, however, have considered that Augustine, though he did publish some good material, has a great deal to answer for. I am one such.

I have already used two words that need explanation: *ekklēsia* and Christendom. Here's a simple definition of each.

---

[1] I have cribbed my title from John Maynard Keynes, who, in July 1925, wrote a pamphlet entitled 'The Economic Consequences of Mr Churchill', but all similarity with that work ends here.
[2] See, for instance, Stuart Murray: *Post-Christendom*, Paternoster, Carlisle, 2004.

By *ekklēsia*, I mean – as the Greek states – those who are called out of the world, separated from the world, to be united to Christ. These called-out ones come together, agree together to submit to the Lord Christ in obedience to his law. They are the children of the new covenant. This is what the New Testament means by the *ekklēsia*.

By Christendom, I mean that political-religious corporation brought into existence by the shenanigans of the Fathers in cahoots with the Roman emperors, Constantine (ruled 306-337) and Theodosius (ruled 379-395). The tortuous manoeuvrings of these politicians, writers, teachers, theologians, preachers and opinion-formers produced the monstrosity of Christendom, leading to the unscriptural notions of belonging to a Christian country, State religion, clericalism, priestcraft, sacramentalism and sacerdotalism, infant baptism and infant regeneration, church buildings, sacred space, church attendance, worship services, and so on.[3] Churchianity and Christendom Christians had been born. Christendom lives and thrives – what an oxymoron – to this day.

* * *

Now for those three consequences I spoke of with regard to Augustine's part in the drastic changes brought about by the move from the scriptural *ekklēsia* to the Christendom Church. No doubt a serious chicken-and-egg debate could be held: did Augustine's work cause the change from *ekklēsia* to church, or did he provide the theology needed to bolster those changes? My own view is that while sole responsibility for the changes themselves does not rest with Augustine, even so he is the man who constructed a theology to undergird the various aspects of those changes, and as such he bears a huge responsibility for the resulting damage.

---

[3] For this, and all my claims in this articles, see my *The Pastor*; *Infant*; *Battle*; *Relationship Evangelism*; *The Priesthood of All Believers*; *Priesthood*; *Public Worship: God-Ordained or Man-Invented?*; *Public Worship Notes*; 'Census Shock!'

## 1. Defining those who belong

Augustine taught that the parable of the wheat and tares (Matt. 13:24-30,37-43) means that the church is composed of both believers and unbelievers. He was wrong! Christ did not say the field in which the wheat and tares grow is the church; it is the world. The church is a separate body in the world but called out of the world. Nevertheless Calvin adopted Augustine's interpretation – that the church is mixed, believers and unbelievers – and the Reformed churches have followed him. As for non-Reformed evangelicals, *de facto* an inclusive comprehensiveness is fast becoming the norm. This past fifty years, evangelical opinion-formers have been consulting pagans and adopting their aims, principles and practices to attract attenders to church services, hold them and then coach them into at least a mental assent to truth and some kind of conformity to it in practice. Consequently and overwhelmingly the church is becoming more and more removed from the *ekklēsia* increasingly to become a conglomeration made up of some believers and a growing number of Christendom Christians, with a rump of unbelievers.[4] Before long, the number of true believers will be swamped by the sheer weight of numbers of Christendom Christians, not to say, rank unbelievers, which they have so strenuously sought to attract.

## 2. Increase by coercion

Augustine turned to another parable – that of the Great Banquet – and interpreted 'compel them to come in' (Luke 14:23) literally. In other words, he argued that increase in church attendance and conformity should, if necessary be by coercion. Modern evangelicals have largely dropped the coercion bit, moving from stick to carrot, and using entertainment (in the widest sense) to attract attenders. I used the word 'largely' in 'largely dropped coercion'. Coercion is not entirely forgotten today. The Reformed who subscribe to – submit to – the 1647 Westminster documents, still hold to these words:

---

[4] See my 'Census Shock!' on my sermonaudio.com page.

The civil magistrate... hath authority, and it is his duty, to take order, that unity and peace be preserved in the Church, that the truth of God be kept pure and entire; that all blasphemies and heresies be suppressed; all corruptions and abuses in worship and discipline prevented or reformed; and all the ordinances of God duly settled, administrated and observed. For the better effecting whereof, he hath power to call synods, to be present at them, and to provide that whatsoever is transacted in them be according to the mind of God.

In this, the men of Westminster were following Calvin:

God gives us leave to endeavour as much as is possible for us to bring them back again which are out of the way of salvation... Magistrates are armed with the sword, to punish those whom God brings to their hands, and to put this doctrine in use.[5]

What is more, a considerable number of evangelicals who do not necessarily subscribe to Westminster, while they have dropped Augustine's position on coercion, nevertheless are looking to the State to encourage – enforce – pagans to conform outwardly to biblical practice. Leaving aside, for now, the unscriptural, non-new-covenant nature of this, have evangelicals considered what if – which, in the UK, does not seem to be a remote possibility – the State becomes Islamic? This departure from Scripture, this defection from the new covenant, will come back to bite the Christendom churches.

### 3. Infant baptism

The New Testament – the new covenant – is clear: in accordance with Christ's command, all those who trust Christ – and only those who trust Christ – are to be dipped – immersed, plunged – in water to symbolise their union to Christ in his death and resurrection, their spiritual death to the old life, their resurrection to the new, and the removal of all their sin in the

---

[5] John Calvin: 'First Sermon Upon the Seventh Chapter' in *Sermons on Deuteronomy*.

blood of Christ. Baptism accomplishes none of this, of course,[6] but it does symbolise it.

Augustine, by philosophical arguments, worked out a complicated theology to justify the growing practice of infant baptism. His main tenet was that the sprinkling of babies by a professional cleric actually removed original sin. Without it the infant would be damned.

While the Reformed have tweaked Augustine's doctrine, their tortuous covenant theology still preserves the notion of baptismal regeneration. For many Christendom Christians, infant baptism makes the baby a Christian.

In addition, many evangelicals who reject infant baptism are growing indifferent to it. As for believer's baptism, it is not unknown for it to degenerate into a rite of passage into adulthood, a sort of social gala with echoes of an American graduation celebration conducted in a party atmosphere. Christendom churches are increasingly tolerant of a range of views on baptism.

*The upshot*

A stark choice is before us: either we stick with what the last 1600 years of Christendom has produced, and continues to develop, or we flee from Babylon (2 Cor. 6:14 – 7:1; Rev. 18:4), and work and look for a measure of recovery of the life of the *ekklēsia*. If we take the former route, we will find that Christendom will exact its pound of flesh. If we take the latter route... well, that will take us to the New Testament way of suffering with and for Christ.

---

[6] See my *Baptist Sacramentalism.*

# Begg on Baptism: Playing with Fire

I wish I didn't have to write this article, but the issue is so important...

But talk about David and Goliath! What gives this virtual nonentity the right to question – let alone strongly disagree with and confront – one of the brightest stars in the galaxy of contemporary evangelical preachers, one who is followed by thousands?

That's the response I expect.

In his discourse, 'The Baptism Debate', Alister Begg, himself, gave me the right.[1] He told us all to emulate the spirit of Acts 17:11. That would have been my position anyway, but that's what he said. So here goes.

I'm not going to repeat my arguments against the double-speaking contradictions of infant baptisers, nor against their dreadful confusion over the covenants, having already set all that out in print.[2]

No! I simply want to point out that Begg, when he delivered that address, was either being remarkably naive or else playing with fire. As I have said, he is followed by thousands, and, as such, his words have influence – for good or ill. The point is, Begg spoke at length on infant baptism, quoting extensively from some of the leading exponents of the practice, and although he showed that he did not altogether buy into their teaching, he was, I am convinced, at the very least, unwise in some of his comments.

---

[1] YouTube 16th Dec. 2022.
[2] See my *Infant*; see also, on my sermonaudio.com page, my 'Reformed Infant Baptismal Regeneration'.

In particular, he talked about believers being 'unnecessarily divided' over 'the meaning and mode of baptism' since, he said, we are 'united on the fundamentals of the gospel'.

I'll say it again: in my view, such talk is highly dangerous. I know it is a growing phenomenon: many Reformed teachers (both Presbyterian and Baptist varieties) are prepared to ease the sprinkling of infants (baby baptism) or dipping of believers into a convenient filing cabinet labelled 'Non-Essentials' – as long as they are agreed on what they call 'the fundamentals'.[3]

But this is nonsense!

Why?

For a start, who in Scripture ever used the concept? I can't imagine the man of Acts 20 chopping the Bible into bits in this way, and putting to one side certain doctrines and practices which his hearers might well regard as ticklish, hoping that the apostle wouldn't mention any of them. Oh no! This is what Paul told the Ephesian elders, and the context in which he told them:

> Therefore I testify to you this day that I am innocent of the blood of all, for I did not shrink from declaring to you the whole counsel of God. Pay careful attention to yourselves and to all the flock, in which the Holy Spirit has made you overseers, to care for the church of God, which he obtained with his own blood. I know that after my departure fierce wolves will come in among you, not sparing the flock; and from among your own selves will arise men speaking twisted things, to draw away the disciples after them. Therefore be alert, remembering that for three years I did not cease night or day to admonish every one with tears (Acts 20:26-31).

And, don't forget, he didn't adopt the notion of 'non-fundamental' when it came to Peter's eating habits (Gal. 2:11-14) – what a heap of personal trouble that would have spared him!

---

[3] See my *False Brothers: Paul and Today* for my comments on John MacArthur and R.C.Sproul.

It seems to me that Paul had never been told of the commandment: 'Thou shalt not rock the boat! Keep the peace at all costs!'

The fact is, defining fundamental and non-fundamental principles of the gospel has proved notoriously elusive. It sounds clever and comforting – in theory; in practice, things are not so easy. Men have certainly tried – Richard Baxter, for one.[4] But they always fail. For one thing, circumstances can alter cases.[5]

Moreover, there is something much more fundamental (pun intended) going on. Let's allow, for sake of argument, that infant sprinkling can be tolerated as 'a non-fundamental', a subject of academic difference and debate. If so, we end up in a place Scripture will never allow us to stand. Scripture always insists that we read God's word to learn, to learn that we might feel, and to learn and feel that we might experience and live out (see Proverbs 1:2-6; 2 Timothy 3:15-17; in truth, the entire Bible). It's the old question of light and/or life. Both, of course, are essential. But just because a man knows the gospel in his head – that is, he has light – if that light is not translated into life transformation, he is still in his sins. In other words, we cannot treat doctrine as a matter of debate, an academic subject. We cannot put what we believe into an insulated box, lock the lid, and forget about it in life. Scripture is unequivocal; in both old and new covenants judgment is according to works (see, for example, Psalm 62:12; Proverbs 24:12; Jeremiah 17:10; 32:19; Matthew 16:27; John 5:28-29; Romans 2:3-6; 2 Corinthians 5:10; 1 Peter 1:17; 4:17-18; Revelation 2:23; 20:11-15; 22:12).[6]

---

[4] See D.Martyn Lloyd-Jones: *The Puritans: Their Origins and Successors*.

[5] I am not adopting the Reformed system and virtually equating circumcision and sprinkling. I am merely making an illustration. Sometimes circumcision seemed indifferent to Paul (Acts 16:3; 1 Cor. 7:19; Gal. 5:6; 6:15); other times, it was fundamental (Acts 15:1-2; Rom. 2:25-29; Gal. 5:2-3).

[6] Salvation is by grace; judgment is of works.

What I am saying is that all this talk about 'fundamentals' is missing the point. Begg made the mistake that a growing number make. Theologians, teachers, preachers, lecturers, writers can talk about infant baptism until the cows come home, using all their armoury of double-speak, get-out clauses, small print, and all the rest, but in the end it's not what the bigwigs pronounce or don't pronounce that matters. It's what's going on in the minds of John and Jennifer Bloggs (or Doe) gathered round the font: it's what they think is happening as their little Johnny or Jenny is sprinkled by the minister pronouncing the correct formula. And I am convinced that very many of them they really do think that 'something has been done' to their little one. *And every infant-baptising minister knows this.*

And here we come to the crux.

For the moment, let us put to one side what the minister thinks, and what the parents think. And let us get a grip on what the babies will come to think. *For, above all, it's what little Johnny or Jenny, as they grow up, will come to think of it – that is really crucial here.*

And from what I have discovered in experience and in my reading around the subject, a great many of those growing children really do think 'something has been done' – that they are right with God because of it.

Consequently, to talk about infant sprinkling as a side-issue is nonsense – dangerous nonsense. And the reason is that infant sprinkling introduces a serious confusion – and, at the very least, encourages the making of a devastating mistake – over a vital issue, an issue of eternal consequence. I am talking about regeneration.

Now I am – myself – prepared to use the word 'fundamental' about regeneration, and for a very good reason: Christ gave me the warrant. As he plainly stated:

> Truly, truly, I say to you, unless one is born again he cannot see the kingdom of God... That which is born of the flesh is flesh, and that which is born of the Spirit is spirit. Do not

marvel that I said to you: 'You must be born again'... (John 3:3-8).[7]

You can't be more fundamental than that!

Baby sprinkling very, very seriously jeopardises what people think of regeneration. And that's putting mildly!

I know that the officiating minister can do as Begg did and insist that regeneration is essential, and that the sprinkling has not regenerated the baby – although the words the minister uses often get very close to it, if not actually asserting it.[8] But if the minister has sprinkled a baby with the appropriate form of covenant-theology double-speak – I make no apology for such language[9] – I am convinced that the overwhelming majority of parents who have used the minister's ministrations – *along with their growing infants* – do rely on his actions and words at the font, and quietly ignore all his warnings and get-out clauses.

For such ministers, doling out categorical, glowing promises – as it were – with the right hand, and taking them back with the left, all of it couched in a tortuous theology, leaving the *hoi polloi* free to pick and choose, preferring 'the nice bits', might, they think, let them off the hook. If so, it's not only the parents and the growing babies who have got it terribly wrong, and are accountable. The ministers are fooling themselves. And they will have to carry the can for their part in the débacle!

---

[7] Christ used 'water' in 'unless one is born of water and the Spirit' (John 3:5) as an illustration of cleansing, renewal. He was not referring to water baptism (see my *Infant*; *Baptist Sacramentalism*).

[8] As above, see my 'Reformed Infant Baptismal Regeneration'.

[9] See my *Infant*.

# Believers One and All

All men and women are believers; not just Christians. Yes, even atheists are believers. Indeed, all men and women are believers on the questions which matter most. The fundamental questions are not, as so many think, how this planet, this universe, has developed to its present state of complexity, and such like. Oh no! It is not whether Charles Darwin was right or wrong. That's only tinkering at the edges. We need to go much deeper. And we do! And it's precisely at this point, that all of us, without exception, are in the same boat: we are all believers, and nothing but believers.

Let me explain.

1. The existence of God. The Christian believes that God exists: 'In the beginning, God...' (Gen. 1:1) 'Whoever would draw near to God must believe that he exists' (Heb. 11:6). The atheist believes there is no god. Neither the Christian nor the atheist can prove his claim or disprove the other's. It is all a question of faith. Thus, both the Christian and the atheist are believers.

G.K.Chesterton:

> When men choose not to believe in God, they do not thereafter believe in nothing. They then become capable of believing in anything.

Let's see if Chesterton was right.

2. God created the universe. The Christian believes that 'in the beginning, God created the heavens and the earth' (Gen. 1:1). 'The builder of all things is God' (Heb. 3:4). The atheist believes that the universe just came into existence spontaneously. Neither the Christian nor the atheist can prove his claim or disprove the other's. It is all a question of faith. Thus, both the Christian and the atheist are believers.

3. God created life. The Christian believes that God created life itself, the life of man in particular: 'The LORD God formed the

man of dust from the ground and breathed into his nostrils the breath of life, and the man became a living creature' (Gen. 2:7). The atheist believes that life arose as a result of spontaneous self-generation, or by 'panspermia' – an unmanned spacecraft bringing it to earth from outer space, where it had arisen spontaneously. Neither the Christian nor the atheist can prove his claim or disprove the other's. It is all a question of faith. Thus, both the Christian and the atheist are believers.

4. God will judge the world by the Lord Jesus Christ. The Christian believes that 'it is appointed for man to die once, and after that comes judgment' (Heb. 9:27), and that God 'has fixed a day on which he will judge the world in righteousness by a man whom he has appointed; and of this he has given assurance to all by raising him from the dead' (Acts 17:31). The atheist believes there is no life after death and no judgment. Neither the Christian nor the atheist can prove his claim or disprove the other's. It is all a question of faith. Thus, both the Christian and the atheist are believers.

So let's have no more atheistical claptrap dismissing the Christian as a man of faith, while exalting the atheist as a man of reason, one who disdains the childish notion of faith. On these cardinal questions, both the Christian and the atheist are believers.

Moreover, it should put a stop to atheistical cant and arrogance. The atheist should face the fact that he might be wrong, and think of the consequences if he is. The Christian does – will the atheist?

Paul did:

> If there is no resurrection of the dead, then not even Christ has been raised. And if Christ has not been raised, then our preaching is in vain and your faith is in vain. We are even found to be misrepresenting God, because we testified about God that he raised Christ, whom he did not raise if it is true that the dead are not raised. For if the dead are not raised, not even Christ has been raised. And if Christ has not been raised, your faith is futile and you are still in your sins. Then those

also who have fallen asleep in Christ have perished. If in Christ we have hope in this life only, we are of all people most to be pitied (1 Cor. 15:13-19).

So, I say to every atheist: ask yourself three questions: Whence, Why and Whither.

Whence? That is, where did life – my life – come from? How did life itself begin?

Why? That is, what is it all about, what is the point, why do I exist?

Whither? That is, what is the end of it all – for me?

# Paul's Breathtaking Assertion

Paul was desperately worried about the Galatian believers; they were listening to the teaching of false brothers, the *pseudadelphoi*. Worse still, they were accepting the so-called gospel that the *pseudadelphoi* were preaching – a 'gospel' which was no gospel at all. So great was his concern, the apostle wrote to the Galatians, and, pulling no punches, he let them know just how serious their defection was, and just how foolish – sinful – they were being:

> I am astonished [he thundered] that you are so quickly deserting him who called you in the grace of Christ and are turning to a different gospel – not that there is another one, but there are some who trouble you and want to distort the gospel of Christ. But even if we or an angel from heaven should preach to you a gospel contrary to the one we preached to you, let him be accursed. As we have said before, so now I say again: If anyone is preaching to you a gospel contrary to the one you received, let him be accursed (Gal. 2:6-9).

In order to make sure his point got home, the apostle reminded his readers what they (and he includes himself), as believers, had been before conversion, how dire their natural spiritual state had been, and how glorious a change they had experienced:

> We..., when we were children [that is, when we were immature; that is, before our conversion – DG], were enslaved to the elementary principles of the world. But when the fullness of time had come, God sent forth his Son, born of woman, born under the law, to redeem those who were under the law, so that we might receive adoption as sons. And because you are sons, God has sent the Spirit of his Son into our hearts, crying, 'Abba! Father!'

Having laid this foundation, the apostle went on, now confining his remarks to the Galatian believers, taking them back over their experience, reminding them of what had happened to them, expanding on the dramatic alteration in their condition:

So you are no longer a slave, but a son, and if a son, then an heir through God. Formerly, when you did not know God, you were enslaved to those that by nature are not gods. But now that you have come to know God, or rather to be known by God...

I break in. Don't miss the apostle's 'but now'. They had been slaves, slaves of false gods, utterly ignorant of God. But they had been converted, and, now, being sons of the one and only true God, slaves of Christ (Rom. 6:16-20; 1 Cor. 6:19-20; 7:22-23; Col. 1:7; 2 Tim. 2:24; 1 Pet. 2:16), they are no longer slaves of false gods. And yet – 'but now' – he thundered, despite that glorious change, and acting directly contradictory to it, the Galatians were adopting the pernicious teaching of the false brothers – the *pseudadelphoi* – and going back into slavery! Can you credit it!

Paul, pleading with the Galatian believers not to listen to the *pseudadelphoi*, set his readers' conversion in its proper context. They have come to know God – or rather, as he said, been known by God; that is, by the predestinating grace of God, on the basis of the free, electing grace of God, manifested in the redemption which Christ accomplished, applied by the sovereign Spirit, the Galatians had been converted, had been redeemed, had been delivered from slavery. And all was by God's free and sovereign grace.

In light of this, he came to the unthinkable:

> But now that you have come to know God, or rather to be known by God, how can you turn back again to the weak and worthless elementary principles of the world, whose slaves you want to be once more? You observe days and months and seasons and years! I am afraid I may have laboured over you in vain (Gal. 4:3-11).

After their remarkable deliverance, the Galatian believers were leaving Christ and going back into slavery.[1] I repeat my question, therefore. Can you credit it! Going back under law,

---

[1] The writer of Hebrews was concerned with the same thing among converted Jews.

returning to their former way of thinking and living, spelled slavery and meant disaster. And that's precisely what the Galatian believers were doing: forsaking grace and plunging into bondage.

\* \* \*

We need to be clear about what this involved.

We know that the *pseudadelphoi* were pushing the Mosaic law, doing the same in Galatia as they had done in Antioch:

> Some men came down from Judea [to Antioch] and were teaching the brothers: 'Unless you are circumcised according to the custom of Moses, you cannot be saved' (Acts 15:1).

As I say, these teachers had now shown up in Galatia, bent on pedalling their false gospel there; and that was why Paul gave his readers a résumé of his own painful experience of these men (Gal. 2:1-14).

Once again, we need to be precise.

As I have argued elsewhere, 'unless you are circumcised' is shorthand for 'unless you come under the Mosaic law'; as the apostle explained: 'I testify again to every man who accepts circumcision that he is obligated to keep the whole law' (Gal. 5:3). You can't pick and choose with the law; it's all or nothing.

What is more, 'you cannot be saved' cannot be confined to justification. It includes that, of course, but it also includes progressive sanctification.[2] Reading through the entire book of Galatians confirms the point. And progressive sanctification is the nub of the issue which concerned Paul in Galatians 4 – indeed throughout the letter, especially from Galatians 3:1 and on. Justification? Yes, of course; but progressive sanctification is key.[3] Without justification, no sinner can be saved – no

---

[2] See my *False Brothers: Paul and Today*; 'Getting Galatians Right' in my *New-Covenant Articles Volume Thirteen*; *Sanctification in Galatians*.

[3] See the previous note. See also my *Christ Is All*.

question of it! But the same goes for progressive sanctification; without progressive sanctification, no sinner will be saved. 'Holiness without which no one will see the Lord' (Heb. 12:14), is how the writer to the Hebrews put it. And if anybody should try to relegate this to justification or positional sanctification, let him read the context:

> [God] disciplines us for our good, that we may share his holiness. For the moment all discipline seems painful rather than pleasant, but later it yields the peaceful fruit of righteousness to those who have been trained by it. Therefore lift your drooping hands and strengthen your weak knees, and make straight paths for your feet, so that what is lame may not be put out of joint but rather be healed. Strive for peace with everyone, and for the holiness without which no one will see the Lord. See to it that no one fails to obtain the grace of God; that no 'root of bitterness' springs up and causes trouble, and by it many become defiled; that no one is sexually immoral or unholy like Esau, who sold his birthright for a single meal. For you know that afterward, when he desired to inherit the blessing, he was rejected, for he found no chance to repent, though he sought it with tears (Heb. 12:10-17).

If that isn't progressive sanctification – personal holiness of life – nothing is! What is more, the context does not start at Hebrews 12:12. Read from Hebrews 12:1. Go back to Hebrews 11:1. Indeed, do as the writer did and start at Hebrews 1:1.

And Paul spelled out the unbreakable connection between justification and progressive sanctification:

> Now that you have been set free from sin and have become slaves of God, the fruit you get leads to [progressive] sanctification and its end, eternal life. For the wages of sin is death, but the free gift of God is eternal life in Christ Jesus our Lord (Rom. 6:22).

Indeed, the reading of Galatians 4:9 to the end of the book, confirms that, in his argument with the Galatians consequent to his expostulation about the freeness of grace in conversion, apart from a brief mention of justification (Gal. 5:4-6), Paul's concern was with progressive sanctification. 'Running well... obeying the truth... serve... walk by the Spirit... works... live by the Spirit... keep in step with the Spirit... sows to the Spirit... doing good... do good... walk...' (Gal. 5:7,13,16,19,25; 6:8,9,10,16) are not words of justification but of progressive sanctification. And the apostle, in his drive for progressive sanctification, never called for any return to the Mosaic law, but insisted on submission to the law of Christ (Gal. 6:2).[4]

* * *

The truth is, the Galatian believers, by listening to the *pseudadelphoi* with their call for submission to the Mosaic law, were actually going back to their former slavery.

And it's here that we run smack into a problem.

The Galatians – being Gentiles – were never under the Mosaic law. The law was given to Israel, and to Israel only, given by God to Israel as his own special people, marking them out from all others (Deut. 4:6-45; 5:26; 7:6-11; Ps. 147:19-20; Rom. 9:4). Take the sabbath, for instance. The sabbath was given, not to Gentiles, but to the Jews through Moses (Ex. 31:12-17; Neh. 9:14; Ezek. 20:12). It was a central part of God's covenant with Israel, his special people (Deut. 4:1-8,44-45; 5:1-3; 29:1,10-15,25,29).[5] God gave the Jews a special – unique – sign that they were his people. This sign belonged to no other people, since only Israel was his nation. And this sign was his sabbaths: 'Moreover I also gave them my sabbaths, to be a sign between them and me, that they might know that I am the LORD who sanctifies them' (Ezek. 20:12); that is, separates them from all other peoples. God commanded the Jews 'to hallow my sabbaths, and they will be a sign between me and you, that you may know that I am the LORD your God' (Ezek. 20:20). And the same applied to their following generations (Ex. 31:13). By 'sabbaths', of course, God meant the weekly sabbaths in

---

[4] For more on this, see my 'Free Grace: Liberty & Duty' on my sermonaudion.com page.

[5] The words 'him who is not here with us today' (Deut. 29:14-15) refer to the descendants of the children of Israel, not to all the rest of the human race.

particular. In short, God commanded Israel from that time on to keep his law – including the sabbath – *especially the sabbath – as a sign that they were God's nation, distinct from all others*:

> Surely my sabbaths you shall keep, for it is a sign between me and you throughout your generations, that you may know that it is the LORD who sanctifies you. You shall keep the sabbath, therefore, for it is holy to you. Everyone who profanes it shall surely be put to death... Work shall be done for six days, but the seventh is the sabbath of rest, holy to the LORD. Whoever does any work on the sabbath day, he shall surely be put to death. Therefore the children of Israel shall keep the sabbath, to observe the sabbath throughout their generations as a perpetual covenant. It is a sign between me and the children of Israel for ever; for in six days the LORD made the heavens and the earth, and on the seventh day he rested and was refreshed (Ex. 31:13-17).

And the Galatians were not Jews! What is more, even here in Galatians Paul talked about them as believers going back to the old pagan laws. In their former state, they had been:

> ...enslaved to the elementary principles of the world... you were enslaved to those that by nature are not gods.

In Christ, they had been delivered, redeemed, liberated, set free. Consequently, Paul thundered:

> How can you turn back again to the weak and worthless elementary principles of the world, whose slaves you want to be once more? You observe days and months and seasons and years! I am afraid I may have laboured over you in vain.

Clearly this bondage might have involved Jewish days, probably did involve Jewish days and rituals, but it certainly involved pagan days, pagan rituals, pagan rules, pagan thinking.

So what's the problem?

Just this. The *pseudadelphoi* were pedalling the Mosaic law. They were not pedalling pagan laws. Some false teachers were, but not, as far as I can see, at Galatia. At Colosse, false teachers *were* prepared to mix Jewish and pagan law. As Paul told the believers there, because of Christ's redemption:

...see to it that no one takes you captive by philosophy and empty deceit, according to human tradition, according to the elemental spirits of the world, and not according to Christ... Therefore let no one pass judgment on you in questions of food and drink, or with regard to a festival or a new moon or a sabbath. These are a shadow of the things to come, but the substance belongs to Christ. Let no one disqualify you, insisting on asceticism and worship of angels, going on in detail about visions, puffed up without reason by his sensuous mind, and not holding fast to the Head, from whom the whole body, nourished and knit together through its joints and ligaments, grows with a growth that is from God.
If [since] with Christ you died to the elemental spirits of the world, why, as if you were still alive in the world, do you submit to regulations 'Do not handle, Do not taste, Do not touch' (referring to things that all perish as they are used) – according to human precepts and teachings? These have indeed an appearance of wisdom in promoting self-made religion and asceticism and severity to the body, but they are of no value in stopping the indulgence of the flesh (Col. 2:8,16-23).

But the false teachers in Galatia were preaching the Mosaic law, and that's what the Galatian believers were buying into. They were submitting to the law of Moses, and, it seems, mixing this with their former paganism. Hence Paul's explosion. How on earth can you think of going back to your former lifestyle and become slaves of law – whether the law of Moses or pagan law – all over again! That's what the apostle found so incredible.

*But this means that Paul was prepared to put the Mosaic law and pagan laws in the same basket, describing both as 'weak and beggarly'.*

Wow! Talk about daring!

As Douglas J.Moo, quoting C.K.Barrett, put it:

This is an incredibly bold claim. Barrett claims that we find here 'as extraordinary a statement as is to be found anywhere in [Paul's] letters... Here in Galatians he virtually equates

Judaism with heathenism. To go forward into Judaism is to go backward into heathenism'.[6]

Thus Moo and Barrett.

And what gives all this greater significance is that the apostle makes this connection more-or-less as an aside – always a more telling way of making a point than using a full-blown argument.

What was Paul thinking of in taking such a risk? Nothing less than doing all he can to keep believers from going back into slavery, pulling out all the stops, throwing caution to the winds; that's what he was doing here.

Moo again:

> Paul is pulling out all the rhetorical stops to convince the Galatians not to take what he views as a disastrous step [too weak: it was disastrous – DG]. To accomplish this, he implies that putting themselves under the law, since the era of the law has ended with the coming of the promised Seed [Christ], is akin to returning to their impotent pagan religions.[7]

His animated language is on a par with the way he expressed his passionate attitude towards unconverted Jews:

I am speaking the truth in Christ – I am not lying; my conscience bears me witness in the Holy Spirit – that I have great sorrow and unceasing anguish in my heart. For I could wish that I myself were accursed and cut off from Christ for the sake of my brothers, my kinsmen according to the flesh... Brothers, my heart's desire and prayer to God for them is that they may be saved... Now I am speaking to you Gentiles. Inasmuch then as I am an apostle to the Gentiles, I magnify my ministry in order somehow to make my fellow-Jews jealous, and thus save some of them (Rom. 9:1-3; 10:1; 11:13-14).[8]

Paul explained where the Jews went wrong:

---

[6] Douglas J.Moo: *Galatians*, Baker Academic, Grand Rapids, 2013, p277, quoting C.K.Barrett: *Freedom and Obligation: A Study of... Galatians*.

[7] Moo p277.

[8] See my *Romans 11*.

Israel who pursued a law that would lead to righteousness [that is, if they could keep it perfectly – DG] did not succeed in reaching that law. Why? Because they did not pursue it by faith, but as if it were based on works. They have stumbled over the stumbling stone, as it is written: 'Behold, I am laying in Zion a stone of stumbling, and a rock of offence; and whoever believes in him [Christ] will not be put to shame'.
Brothers, my heart's desire and prayer to God for them is that they may be saved. For I bear them witness that they have a zeal for God, but not according to knowledge. For, being ignorant of the righteousness of God, and seeking to establish their own, they did not submit to God's righteousness. For Christ is the end of the law for righteousness to everyone who believes.
For Moses writes about the righteousness that is based on the law, that the person who does the commandments shall live by them. But the righteousness based on faith says... (Rom. 9:31 – 10:6).

I agree that the apostle was speaking about justification in that extract, but it is his attitude that I am concerned with. Above all, it was the way he spoke about the Mosaic law that I wanted to bring out.

And the apostle had just showed similar daring, being even more blunt, when he told the believers in Rome that:

God [in Christ] has done what the law, weakened by the flesh, could not do (Rom. 8:3).

Paul was not alone in showing such boldness and freeness, of course. Take the writer to the Hebrews; because of Christ's redeeming work, and his bringing in of the new covenant, the writer was prepared to say that the old covenant is now 'obsolete' (Heb. 8:13). As he had just said:

A former commandment is set aside because of its weakness and uselessness (for the law made nothing perfect); but on the other hand, a better hope is introduced, through which we draw near to God (Heb. 7:18-19).

Take Peter; he, too, was not afraid to call a spade a spade:

They [that is, false teachers] promise them freedom, but they themselves are slaves of corruption. For whatever overcomes a person, to that he is enslaved. For if, after they have escaped the defilements of the world through the knowledge of our Lord and Saviour Jesus Christ, they are again entangled in them and overcome, the last state has become worse for them than the first. For it would have been better for them never to have known the way of righteousness than after knowing it to turn back from the holy commandment [that is, the gospel – DG] delivered to them. What the true proverb says has happened to them: 'The dog returns to its own vomit, and the sow, after washing herself, returns to wallow in the mire' (2 Pet. 2:19-22).

You can't get it much stronger than that!

John put it succinctly:

The law was given through Moses; grace and truth came through Jesus Christ (John 1:17).

And it Paul's linking of the Mosaic law and pagan law that's the breathtaking assertion of my title.

\* \* \*

We must never play this down! Never! But all too often it is played down and explained away. And doing that is not only wrong; it grievously diminishes the glorious grace of God in the gospel. In fact, it destroys the essence of the new covenant – free grace. It detracts from the work of the Spirit – which is to glorify Christ (John 16:14).

How is Paul's argument played down and explained away?

The Reformed have two ways round the apostle's argument. *First*, they say it only concerns justification. *Secondly*, they divide the law into three and say the apostle does not include the moral law in all this, but confines his strictures to the ceremonial or judicial law. Both tricks – and that's what they are, nothing but tricks – may be clever, but they are utterly unscriptural, and simply do not fit the context. And we need to remember that God requires us not to be smart but scriptural.

Why do the Reformed do it? For two reasons.

*First*, because of their covenant theology. They feel they must do all they can to make Scripture fit into their system. The slightest questioning of the system, the Confession, must, at all costs, be resisted: 'Touch not the Confession' seems to be their mantra, accommodating 1 Chronicles 16:22.

*Secondly*, fear. Fear? Yes, fear. There are two parts to this: (a) they have adopted John Calvin's threefold use of the law and thus look upon the law as a whip. As he put it:

> The law acts like a whip to the flesh, urging it on as men do to a lazy sluggish ass. Even in the case of a spiritual man, inasmuch as he is still burdened with the weight of the flesh, the law is a constant stimulus, pricking him forward when he would indulge in sloth.[9]

Well, that spells it out. Even the spiritual man needs to have fear instilled in him, and that is brought about by lashing him with the whip: that is, by preaching the law to him.

And (b) fear that free grace – and that is precisely what Paul preached – will lead to antinomianism.[10]

So, in order to try to get professing believers to be converted,[11] or, if converted, to live holy lives, the Puritans – the master legal-teachers – concreted their legal system into their Confessions and Catechisms. By preaching law, law, law, they hoped to see sinners convicted – and, thereafter, converted – and, once converted, to see them as saints progressively sanctified.

Contemporary Reformed teachers, following their mentors, instinctively reach out for the law. They argue that we must

---

[9] John Calvin: *Institutes*: 2:7. See my *Christ Is All*.

[10] See my 'The Law and the Confessions' in my *New-Covenant Articles Volume One*; *Four Antinomians Tested*; *John Bunyan*.

[11] A direct result of infant baptism is churches of mixed regenerate and unregenerate. John Calvin's teaching cemented the medieval system. It is a disaster of the first water. See my *Infant*; *Battle*.

preach the law to bring conviction of sin and prepare men for Christ![12] They then argue for justification on the basis of free grace without the law. But – and here's the rub – they immediately go on to claim that progressive sanctification is by the law, and so they preach law to believers. And this is quite wrong.[13]

No! There's nothing for it. Law-teachers today come under Paul's strictures in Galatians, and they – *to use an understatement* – need to have a serious re-think of their covenant theology. We believers need to recover the truth that, from first to last, salvation is by God's free and sovereign grace, and we must never – never – draw back from the liberty Christ has wrought for us by going into bondage of any sort – whether it be Jewish or pagan.

---

[12] See my *Christ Is All*; 'Preparationism in New England' in my *New-Covenant Articles Volume Two*.
[13] See my *Christ Is All*.

# *Census Shock!*

What shock?

On 29th November 2022, BBC reporters Rachel Russell and Harry Farley published an article under the screamer: 'Less than half of England and Wales population Christian, Census 2021 shows'.[1]

Well, in my case the screamer worked – it certainly caught my attention. More, it moved me to write this brief article in reply.

An appalling ignorance – an appalling, fearful delusion – lies (how apt a word!) at the heart of all this. That's the real sadness – sadness, please note, not shock. So serious is this delusion, so far-reaching are its consequences, I publish this piece hoping to un-delude as many as possible.

\* \* \*

The number of Christians in England and Wales in 2021 was just less than thirty million. And that was supposed to be a shock!

Not so! If only! The shock would have been to learn that there really were thirty million Christians in England and Wales! The real sadness – sadness, not shock, I say again – is that anybody – millions, in fact – are deluded enough to have such a woolly, wrong-headed notion of what a 'Christian' is!

And this matters! Eternal issues hang on it.

How do people get into this state? For a start, instead of consulting the maker's manual, men have come up with their own definition, or blindly accepted the definition concocted by others. How foolish!

---

[1] BBC News website 29th Nov. 2022.

When I want to know how something works, or what to do when something goes wrong with some gadget or other – a warning light comes on, whatever – I consult the handbook. Odd though it might seem, I work on the peculiar principle that the manufacturer ought to know how his product works, that he has spelled out what I need to know about the apparatus, and how to use it. Am I unique in this? Do medical practitioners not consult the pharmacopeia? Do court officials not consult legal precedents and laws enacted by Parliament? Or do they make it up as they go along? Do they stick a wetted finger in the air, and lemming-like follow the crowd over the precipice?

It's all to do with this word 'Christian'.

The great essential, surely, is to find out what the Bible means by 'Christian'. Now it may surprise some to learn that although the word 'Christian' is used in the Bible, it isn't used much.

It first saw the light of day, probably as a derogatory nickname or dismissive label stuck on believers by their enemies:

> In Antioch the disciples were first called Christians (Acts 11:26).

Two things stand out: *First*, the disciples did not define themselves with the name – with any name, as far as I can tell; but that was how their enemies tagged them: 'Christians'. *Secondly*, it is clear that the outstanding thing about believers, as far as their enemies were concerned, was their connection with Christ.

The second scriptural use of the word is in Agrippa's dismissive retort to Paul:

> In a short time would you persuade me to be a Christian? (Acts 26:28)

The third time (and the only time by an apostle) is in Peter's first letter:

> If anyone suffers as a Christian, let him not be ashamed, but let him glorify God in that name. For it is time for judgment to begin at the household of God; and if it begins with us, what

will be the outcome for those who do not obey the gospel of God? (1 Pet. 4:16-17).

This unique reference must serve as the main source for our understanding of what a Christian is. Clearly, in those days, being known as a 'Christian' would mark you out as godly, different from the world, separated from pagan culture and its idols, and – far from it being a socially-acceptable tag – being known as a 'Christian' would have spelled trouble for you, and trouble with a capital T.

But with the invention of Christendom, things changed. And how! Since that time, use of 'Christian' has – like Topsy – mushroomed,[2] 'Christian' being larded over with ever-thickening layers of confusion, distortion and downright error, all as direct consequence of Christendom. Christendom? That political-religious corporation brought into existence by the shenanigans of the Fathers in cahoots with the Roman emperors, Constantine and Theodosius. The tortuous manoeuvrings of these politicians, writers, teachers, theologians, preachers and opinion-formers produced the monstrosity of Christendom, leading to the unscriptural notions of belonging to a Christian country, State religion, clericalism, priestcraft, sacramentalism and sacerdotalism, infant baptism and infant regeneration, church buildings, sacred space, church attendance, worship services, and so on.[3] Churchianity and Christendom-Christians had been born. Christendom lives and thrives – what an oxymoron – to this day.

Listen to the sort of nonsense which Christendom has spawned and which people trot out as their definition of being a Christian. One of these might be yours:

'I was born in, and belong to, a Christian country'.

---

[2] The slave girl, when asked where she came from, replied: 'I 'spect I growed' (Harriet Beecher Stowe: *Uncle Tom's Cabin*, 1851). The idiom is often applied today to the sprawl of bloated corporations.
[3] See my *The Pastor*; *Infant*; *Relationship Evangelism Exposed*; *The Priesthood of All Believers*; *Priesthood*.

'My parents were Christians and I was christened as an infant, the minister duly pronouncing I was regenerate, a child of God, under the covenant, or declaring that he had sprinkled me because I was born under the covenant – or somesuch. Whatever, I am a Christian, and have been such from birth'.[4]

'I go to church'.

'I am religious'.

'I am decent, sincere, respectable, live by Christ's ethic'.

'I went to public school,[5] and have adopted the Christian ethic I was taught there'.

'I play the game, especially cricket, keeping a straight bat'.

'I keep the Christian festivals'.

'I think Jesus was a good man'.

'I do my best – what more can you want?'

\* \* \*

As to that last, it's not what I want: it's what the Creator demands.

Let's get down to brass tacks.

I quoted Peter (1 Pet. 4:16-17). I said it must be the starting point for our investigation of 'Christian'. Read his letter and you'll soon get the point. He wrote to people he called 'Christian'. Very well. What did he mean by it? He was writing:

> ...to those who are elect... according to the foreknowledge of God the Father, in the sanctification of the Spirit, for obedience to Jesus Christ and for sprinkling with his blood... Blessed be

---

[4] See 'The BBC Gets It Wrong Again' in my *New-Covenant Articles Volume Thirteen*, and on my sermonaudio.com page.

[5] That is, in the UK, a fee-paying private school, often based on a so-called Christian foundation. That, in itself, illustrates how words can change – lose – their meaning.

the God and Father of our Lord Jesus Christ! According to his great mercy, he has caused us to be born again to a living hope through the resurrection of Jesus Christ from the dead, to an inheritance that is imperishable, undefiled, and unfading, kept in heaven for you, who by God's power are being guarded through faith for a salvation ready to be revealed in the last time (1 Pet. 1:1-5).

As he went on to say, such people have:

... purified [their] souls by... obedience to the truth... [having] been born again, not of perishable seed but of imperishable, through the living and abiding word of God (1 Pet. 1:22-23).

Peter recognised that they had:

...come to [Christ] [that is, they were trusting Christ as Saviour and Lord], a living stone rejected by men but in the sight of God chosen and precious, [and consequently,] you yourselves like living stones are being built up as a spiritual house, to be a holy priesthood, to offer spiritual sacrifices acceptable to God through Jesus Christ... Unto you therefore which believe [Christ] is precious (1 Pet. 2:4-7).

As Peter described them:

You are a chosen race, a royal priesthood, a holy nation, a people for his own possession, that you may proclaim the excellencies of him who called you out of darkness into his marvellous light. Once you were not a people, but now you are God's people; once you had not received mercy, but now you have received mercy (1 Pet. 2:9-10).

Now these are the terms – the scriptural terms – which must be understood about a Christian. This is what we must mean when we use the word 'Christian': Christians are elect, regenerate, believing, separated, washed in Jesus blood, righteous in him; they are those to whom Christ is precious.

Indeed, as Paul put it, a Christian is someone to whom:

...Christ is all, and in all (Col. 3:11).

Much more could be said, but I want to set out the core truth.

The first great essential is regeneration:

Truly, truly, I say to you, unless one is born again he cannot see the kingdom of God... Truly, truly, I say to you, unless one is born of water[6] and the Spirit, he cannot enter the kingdom of God. That which is born of the flesh is flesh, and that which is born of the Spirit is spirit. Do not marvel that I said to you: 'You must be born again'. The wind blows where it wishes, and you hear its sound, but you do not know where it comes from or where it goes. So it is with everyone who is born of the Spirit (John 3:3-8).

I will sprinkle clean water on you, and you shall be clean from all your uncleannesses, and from all your idols I will cleanse you. And I will give you a new heart, and a new spirit I will put within you. And I will remove the heart of stone from your flesh and give you a heart of flesh. And I will put my Spirit within you, and cause you to walk in my statutes and be careful to obey my rules (Ezek. 36:25-27; see also Ezek. 11:19-20).

Anyone who does not have the Spirit of Christ does not belong to him (Rom. 8:9).

Regeneration by the Spirit always leads to repentance, which is essential:

Unless you repent, you will all likewise perish... unless you repent, you will all likewise perish (Luke 13:3,5).

[God] commands all people everywhere to repent (Acts 17:30).

When the sinners who were convicted of sin under Peter's preaching on the day of Pentecost cried out as to what they should do, Peter replied at once:

Repent and be baptised every one of you in the name of Jesus Christ for the forgiveness of your sins (Acts 2:37-38).

Repentance is always accompanied by saving faith, trust in Christ, reliance upon him and his finished work. Paul preached the gospel:

...testifying both to Jews and to Greeks of repentance toward God and of faith in our Lord Jesus Christ (Acts 20:21).

---

[6] This is not baptism. The illustration speaks of washing, cleansing from sin, and which is explained by the next two extracts.

...that they should repent and turn to God (Acts 26:20).

God so loved the world, that he gave his only Son, that whoever believes in him should not perish but have eternal life. For God did not send his Son into the world to condemn the world, but in order that the world might be saved through him. Whoever believes in him is not condemned, but whoever does not believe is condemned already, because he has not believed in the name of the only Son of God (John 3:16-18).

When the Philippian jailer cried out, asking how he could be saved, Paul and Silas replied:

Believe in the Lord Jesus, and you will be saved (Acts 16:30-31).

Paul was categorical:

Everyone who calls on the name of the Lord will be saved (Rom. 10:13).

How does all this dovetail? Like this:

To all who did receive [Christ], who believed in his name, he gave the right to become children of God, who were born, not of blood nor of the will of the flesh nor of the will of man, but of God (John 1:12-13).

All that the Father gives me will come to me, and whoever comes to me I will never cast out... No one can come to me unless the Father who sent me draws him. And I will raise him up on the last day. It is written in the prophets: 'And they will all be taught by God'. Everyone who has heard and learned from the Father comes to me (John 6:37,44-45).

On the last day of the feast, the great day, Jesus stood up and cried out: 'If anyone thirsts, let him come to me and drink. Whoever believes in me, as the Scripture has said, 'Out of his heart will flow rivers of living water'. Now this he said about the Spirit, whom those who believed in him were to receive, for as yet the Spirit had not been given, because Jesus was not yet glorified (John 7:37-39).

When [the Spirit] comes, he will convict the world concerning sin... because they do not believe in me (John 16:8-9).

47

\* \* \*

The notion that in 2021 the number of sinners in England and Wales who were regenerate, convicted of sin, converted to Christ in saving repentance and trust, and found Christ precious and all in all, had dropped to just less than 50%, and that this is headline news, shows, once again,[7] just how far removed from reality the BBC has drifted. But, to be fair, since the monstrosity of Christendom has assumed so dominant a position in the West, nothing less can be expected. The idea that 'Christendom Christians' are real Christians is so far removed from reality that words fail. But as I have said, getting this wrong carries eternal consequences. Unless a sinner is truly converted to Christ, he will die as he was born – under the wrath of God (Rom. 1:18-32; Eph. 2:1-3). And eternal damnation is, in that case, inevitable.

May these words awaken many to call on Christ in saving trust, and so become real Christians.

As William Gadsby put it:

*Pause, my soul! and ask the question,*
*Art thou ready to meet God?*
*Am I made a real Christian,*
*Washed in the Redeemer's blood?*
*Have I union*
*With the church's living Head?*

*Am I quickened by his Spirit;*
*Live a life of faith and prayer?*
*Trusting wholly to his merit;*
*Casting on him all my care?*
*Daily panting,*
*In his likeness to appear?*

*If my hope on Christ is stayèd,*
*Let him come when he thinks best;*
*O my soul! be not dismayèd,*
*Lean upon his loving breast;*

---

[7] As before, see 'The BBC Gets It Wrong Again' in my *New-Covenant Articles Volume Thirteen*, and on my sermonaudio.com page.

## Census Shock!

*He will cheer thee*
*With the smilings of his face.*

*But, if still a total stranger*
*To his precious name and blood,*
*Thou art on the brink of danger;*
*Canst thou face a holy God?*
*Think and tremble,*
*Death is now upon the road.*

# Evangelical Christendom Confusion: Lloyd-Jones, Brencher and Murray, 1966 and All That

I am referring to D.Martyn Lloyd-Jones' Evangelical Alliance address on 18th October 1966, the chapter 'A Grievous Dividing' in John Brencher's 2002 book on Lloyd-Jones,[1] and the chapter "'The Lost Leader'", or "A Prophetic Voice'" in Iain H.Murray's 2008 book on Lloyd-Jones.[2]

Let me say at once that this article is not yet another addition to the pile of books and articles on the whys and wherefores of that fateful October meeting, the events and reasons which led up to it, and the ensuing aftermath – who said (or didn't say) what and why, and what was meant by it, if it was said. Let that be clear right from the start.

My aim is far more basic. To change the figure, I am standing back and taking a wider view, but, sounding contradictory, I am homing in on something which Lloyd-Jones, Brencher and Murray all missed.

Let me explain. There is a fourth character in the cast list of this drama; indeed, the lead character dominating the whole. The character in question, of course, is Christendom; Evangelical Christendom in particular. Hence my title 'Evangelical Christendom Confusion'. Christendom was in the driving seat in 1966. And though there are encouraging signs – flecks of straw in the wind, one might say – that a small but growing number of believers are showing concern about the devastating effects of Christendom, Christendom, alas, shows no sign of giving up its dominant role.

---

[1] John Bencher: *Martyn Lloyd-Jones (1899-1981) and Twentieth-Century Evangelicalism*, Paternoster Press, Carlisle, 2002, pp116-141.
[2] Iain H.Murray: *Lloyd-Jones: Messenger of Grace*, The Banner of Truth Trust, Edinburgh, 2008, pp165-201.

Let me explain further. I am talking about the confusion – the ruinous confusion – that Christendom has imposed on the issues in hand. It did it in 1966; it continues doing it to this day. And this is more than a pity; it is a disaster. In truth, the entire debate foundered before it began, and it foundered because the three proponents I have selected were not really discussing Scripture – though they fundamentally thought they were; the truth is, they were arguing about concepts invented by Christendom and imposed on Scripture. Failing to deal with the vital – absolutely vital – scriptural issues which were involved, they concentrated instead on Christendom concepts. But the scriptural concepts at stake are vital still, never more so than today.

What were those vital issues? What are they now? The three were, and still are: What is the *euaiggelion* (the gospel)? What is the *ekklēsia* (the church)? What is a *Christianos* (a Christian)?

Let me explain why I put the Greek first. We first meet these three words in the New Testament – in Greek. We do not come across them in some theological manual or confession of faith; we meet them in Scripture. And they have specific, scriptural meanings. All three – gospel, church, Christian – may have become everyday terms in English, but, alas, in coming into English they have picked up – and been ruined by – the fourth character, Christendom. Nearly all believers – let alone the world – tend to think of all three – gospel, church and Christian – not as they should – as defined in the new covenant in Scripture – *but as fatally modified by Christendom*. They may not be aware of the drastic influence Christendom has had upon the new covenant – indeed, most believers, in my view have no concept of it – but such is the case.[3]

---

[3] How many professing evangelicals today are fully up to speed on, say, regeneration, and its effect in the transformed life of the convert? In the discussion of Lloyd-Jones' address in the chapters under discussion, see how 'becoming a Christian' becomes confused with 'attending church', 'being baptised (sprinkled as a baby)', 'accepting a creed'.

Consequently the discussion from first to last in 1966 and since was – and continues to be – vitiated by Christendom. The conversation then and now might appear to be about gospel, church and Christian, yes, but, alas, at the time all three were viewed through the lens of Christendom, and all three continue (by most) to be so viewed. The fact is, a proper understanding of, and sticking to – in particular – *ekklēsia* and *Christianos* – would have saved much breath, paper and ink, and great deal of misunderstanding in 1966, and since. But it's far worse than that. Christendom has inevitably led to serious distortion of *euaiggelion*, *ekklēsia* and *Christianos* for many, with calamitous consequences for both believers and unbelievers.

Hence this article.

But I am resolved to be brief. Those who wish to check my allegations about the parts played by Lloyd-Jones, Brencher and Murray must consult the originals.

And it won't take long to see what I mean: all three were concerned with things like visible and invisible church, denominations, associations (and, in at least one case, associations of denominations), tradition, essential and non-essential (primary and secondary) truths. All of which are Christendom-speak, and, therefore, an integral part of the problem. Consequently, the debate which raged then and since has been utterly confounded by this kind of talk. And the losers are, as I have said, the *euaiggelion* (the gospel), the *ekklēsia* (the church), *Christianos* (Christian). And, of course, several other major new-covenant principles and practices have been caught up in the general confusion; such things as: What is scriptural separation? What is scriptural evangelism? Christendom confusion reigns!

In short, the kerfuffle over the events of October 1966, and its aftermath, has served only to make an already utterly confused situation even more confused. The ramifications of the principles of the new covenant – which, alas, many evangelicals are sadly ignorant of – have been even more seriously muffled in the fog of Christendom.

I will not launch into the ramifications of all this now, but I note some of my many works in which I attempt to deal with the issues.[4]

In brief, the discussion should be about the scriptural meaning and practice of the principles of *euaiggelion, ekklēsia, Christianos*, separation and evangelism. If only we could shake ourselves free from Christendom and get back to the new covenant!

---

[4] See my *Christ Is All*; *Relationship Evangelism Exposed*; *The Pastor*; *Infant*; *Public Worship: God-Ordained or Man-Invented?*; *Battle*; *Evangelicals Warned*, and so on.

# The Law of Diminishing Returns

Once upon a time in the land of Happy Dreams, there was a church – the Traditional Church – which woke up to the worrying discovery that it was not attracting attendees and holding them as much as it used to.[1] The management board came up with a solution.

In three parts.

*First*, the name. From now on the church would be known as the Bright Yungthings Community Centre. Much more inviting.

*Secondly*, the management knew that the problem was not really in the name. The truth is, prospective consumers didn't want to be confronted, confronted with their sin, the wrath of God, their utter ruin and helplessness to save themselves, and, above all, the eternal consequence of all that. So, the Bright Yungthings Community Centre would, in future, assure prospective attendees that they were indeed in serious trouble and needed 'salvation', and that Jesus would indeed 'save' them – save them from their fears, anxieties, worries, hang-ups and so on, and give them a sense of personal fulfilment, but as for confronting them with 'difficult' terms like 'sin' and 'the wrath of God', that, from now on, was, if not entirely out of the question, certainly going to be muted. Putting people off by confronting them with unpalatable truths? No more of that!

*Thirdly*, the management consulted pagan organisations which had successfully worked out how to attract consumers – TV, shopping malls, sports organisers, and the like – and cherry-picked the best bits of advice they could lay their hands on.

And so the Bright Yungthings Community Centre set out on its new course. And it worked! It worked a treat! The seats were soon filled, the walls were bulging at the seams...

---

[1] For justification of my approach in this article, see 'The Weapon of Humour' in my *Battle*.

But, alas, as is the way of things, high summer turned to dying autumn, followed by bitter winter in the land of Happy Dreams, and consumers began to drift away from the Bright Yungthings Community Centre.

Why?

The consumers found that the Slicker Community Centre – just a short car-ride down the road – was offering better fare: better coffee, better music, better lighting, and the like. Naturally, since it was the goodies that had attracted them in the first place, many consumers upped-sticks, switched churches, and set about having a happier time in the new place.

But in due course Slicker found the same as Bright Yungthings: despite the excitement, warm ambience, and the coffee on tap, the consumers could never quite shake off the nagging inner conviction that something was seriously wrong – wrong within, wrong within themselves. As much as the repetitive songs might assure them that all was well and that Jesus was offering them personal satisfaction, and as often as the management kept reminding them that they had never had it so good, they could never quite eradicate the truth of God's word. They found that in spite of the razzmatazz, they were experiencing what that word said, and:

> ...they [were showing] that the work of the law is written on their hearts, while their conscience also [was bearing] witness, and their conflicting thoughts [were accusing or even excusing] them [in anticipation of] that day when, according to [the] gospel, God judges the secrets of men by Christ Jesus (Rom. 2:15-16).[2]

No amount of reinforcement from the opposite direction – whether from the stage, the song book, the worship group, the band, or the buzz of the coffee-supping, cookie-crunching chatter – could quite shake off the nagging thought that they were sinners who needed to be saved; saved, not merely made to

---

[2] For the arguments behind my interpretation, see my *Christ Is All* and my 'All Men Under Law'.

feel better about themselves, but really delivered from their sin – its guilt, condemnation, power and presence. They could not put it into words, but they knew it right enough. They felt it.

So much so, notwithstanding all the efforts to make the gospel palatable to the natural man and woman, the customers were nauseated by the relentless stream of psycho-babble washing over them.[3] The continual coffee and cup-cakes, the drumming of the band, the repeating of the songs, the bland, cheesy assurances from the pep talks, and all the rest of it, palled – and worse. And so they threw in the towel. They quitted church altogether and took their custom elsewhere, back to where there would be no Jesus talk. Pagan culture welcomed back those that it had lost.

And thus the churches in the land of Happy Dreams experienced the law of diminishing returns: dumb down the gospel to attract consumers, give the customers what they want, and in so doing you inevitably sow the seeds of your own ruin. The people of the land of Happy Dreams proved the biblical truth:

> God is not mocked, for whatever one sows, that will he also reap. For the one who sows to his own flesh will from the flesh reap corruption, but the one who sows to the Spirit will from the Spirit reap eternal life (Gal. 6:7-8).

---

[3] I get the very strong impression that many evangelicals have been heavily influenced by the way TV pundits commenting on politics, sport, or whatever, spend so much time analysing motives, feelings, fears and all the rest, often trotting out their favourite bit of psycho-babble.

# Flogging a Dead Horse

That's what it feels like – trying to get the Reformed to engage with Scripture on the law without reading it through a Reformed Confession. But... let's try again.

The so-called threefold division of the law is of paramount importance to the advocates of John Calvin's threefold use of the law. It conveniently enables them not only to enforce their chosen part of the law on believers, but to dispose of – skirt round, explain away – any scriptural passage that contradicts their theology. They dare not let it go. If they do, the whole Reformed edifice of covenant theology on the law will crumble about their ears. And they know it. Sadly, it was also stop them coming to a proper understanding of the law, and the liberty the believer has in Christ under his law in the new covenant.

A friend has recently come across another Reformed attempt to justify the unjustifiable by claiming that because Scripture speaks of God's 'statutes... judgments... commandments' (Lev. 26:15 Deut. 6:1-2; 11:1, for example) this means that Reformed theologians are right to divide the law into three parts – moral, ceremonial and judicial. I would like to raise a few things for these teachers to think about.

*First*, it is true that Scripture does use a variety of terms when speaking about the law – but far more than three: 'precepts, commandments, laws, words, covenant, judgments, commands, statutes, testimonies, rulings, rules, instructions, ordinances, decrees', and the like. So why do they add three more? Why not stick to the many scriptural words, and show us, precisely and scripturally, which of the 613 or so commandments are statutes, precepts, commands, judgments, words, or whatever?

*Secondly*, and more importantly, I might say that Scripture is promiscuous in the way it uses its terms when speaking about the old covenant and its laws, commandments, judgments, statutes and so on, using the terms interchangeably, seemingly indiscriminately. Whatever nuances Scripture attaches to these various words it does not warrant us classifying the law into three separate compartments. Such a notion is ridiculous.

At this point, I had intended to quote several passages of Scripture to prove my assertions, but the scriptural usage of these terms, the sheer multiplicity of the terms themselves, the almost indiscriminate way in which they are used, even within one version, coupled with the variety of excellent versions in use... made the task so complicated that I threw in the towel. I can only ask that readers check these – and scores more – passages in their favoured version (and then repeat the task in another version): the result will be a foregone conclusion.

Take Exodus 12 and on, especially, perhaps, Exodus 15:25-26; 24:3-8; 34:10-11; and then, for instance, Leviticus 20:22; 26:15; Deuteronomy 12:28,32; 24:8; 1 Kings 2:3; 6:12; 8:58,61; 9:4; 11:11,33-38; 2 Kings 17:13-16,19,34-38; 18:6,12; 22:8-13; 23:2-3,21,24-25 2 Chronicles 7:17; 19:8-11; 34:30-32; Nehemiah 1:5; Psalms 105:45; Ezekiel 37:24; Hebrews 9:19-22, and so on!

Not only does Scripture mix up the terms it uses to describe the various laws, it also mixes up the various laws which the Reformed like to keep separate. At the end of Leviticus, after God had reminded Israel of a whole host of laws on all sorts of matters, including idolatry, adultery, disrespect for parents, the weekly sabbath, harvest, resting the land every seven years, the year of jubilee with all its regulations for redemption, and so on, Moses recorded: 'These are the statutes and judgements and laws which the LORD made between himself and the children of Israel on Mount Sinai by the hand of Moses... These are the commandments which the LORD commanded Moses for the children of Israel on Mount Sinai' (Lev. 26:46; 27:34). It did not matter whether or not any particular law was found in the ten commandments or the regulations for the tabernacle or the statutes for the ordering of Jewish society. No Jew ever asked which part of the law any commandment came from. It simply would not have crossed his mind. It was all the law of God; the statutes, judgments, commandments were all part and parcel of the one entire, indivisible law of God which he gave to Israel through Moses on Mount Sinai.

Take Numbers 15. The stoning of the man for transgressing the law of the sabbath (Num. 15:32-36) is sandwiched between – on the one hand, the laws of sacrifice and offering for sin (Num. 15:1-31) – and on the other, the sewing of tassels on the corners of garments (Num. 15:37-40), this last to remind the Israelites to 'remember all the commandments of the LORD and do them' (Num. 15:39-40). And the chapter concludes with words remarkably similar to the preface to the ten commandments (Num. 15:41; Ex. 20:2; Deut. 5:6). My point is that *it is impossible to detect any biblical difference in the designation of any of these laws.* Sacrifices, offerings, sabbath and tassels all – *all* – come under the one umbrella: 'Ordinance... law... custom... all these commandments... all that the LORD has commanded you by the hand of Moses... the LORD gave commandment... law... the word of the LORD... his commandment... So, as the LORD commanded Moses, all the congregation [obeyed]... Remember all the commandments of the LORD and do them... remember and do all my commandments' (Num. 15:15-16,22-23,29,31,36,39-40).

Scripture, I repeat, mixes the laws, statutes, commands, judgments, testimonies, precepts, taking them from all over the entire Mosaic covenant, and calling them the law, the covenant. ***But it never heaps them into three neat piles!***

### Conclusion

The attempted justification of the threefold division of the law based on the various terms Scripture uses to fill out the law is artificial. Worse, it smacks of desperation.

Not only that, the scheme is puerile, totally unworthy of any serious reader of Scripture. The merest glance at Scripture shows up the nonsense for what it is (not) worth.[1]

When are the Reformed going to admit that their system is built, not on Scripture, but on a pre-supposed theology? And give it up? And let Scripture be Scripture? Alas, I fear those questions take me back to where we came in, and my title – 'Flogging a Dead Horse'.

---

[1] It reminds me that when I was getting good marks at school, if I disappointed my father with my incompetence, he would tell me that if I was one of the best then he didn't want to see the worst!

# Salvation in Hebrews

I have culled this article from a passage in my *False Brothers: Paul and Today*,[1] gently edited for this present purpose. In that book, because I was dealing with two main passages – 2 Corinthians 11:26 and Galatians 2:4 – and the Judaisers' demand on Gentile believers: 'Unless you are circumcised according to the custom of Moses, you cannot be saved' (Acts 15:2), it was necessary to show that 'salvation' embraces far more than justification. To add some weight to my argument, I took an overview of Hebrews. It is that overview which I now publish as a free-standing article.

\* \* \*

Even though the letter to the Hebrews was not written by Paul, it has an important contribution to make to the way Paul responded to the false brothers – the *pseudadelphoi*. Strictly speaking the writer of Hebrews is not dealing with the *pseudadelphoi* – at least, I can see no evidence of it. As I explained in my *False Brothers*, the *pseudadelphoi* arose as a reaction to the conversion of Gentiles; Hebrews is concerned with the apostasy of Jewish believers, *their* defection from Christ. In order to prevent this, the writer sets out the superiority of the new covenant over the old. He takes the elements of the old – land, sabbath, tabernacle, priesthood, sacrifice, altar, and argues that Christ is the fulfilment, the reality of them all. He takes the old-covenant characters (or pre-old-covenant characters) – prophets, angels, Moses, Joshua, Melchizedek, Aaron – and shows Christ to be superior to them all. 'Christ is all' (Col. 3:11).

But though they may, as it were, circumnavigate in opposite directions (one set tackling Gentile believers; the other, Jewish), both sets of protagonists – and their errors – end up at the same

---

[1] My *False Brothers: Paul and Today*, pp80-93.

point; namely, the adulteration of the new covenant by the old; which inevitably means the ruin of the new covenant. And, as Paul so bluntly told the Galatians, this spells disaster – the replacement of the gospel of our Lord Jesus Christ, the one and only true gospel, with a false gospel, and the lowering of Christ. Consequently, Hebrews, which has more than any other canonical book to say concerning the new covenant and it supersession of the old, has a great deal to tell us about what the writer called 'such a great salvation' (Heb. 2:3) accomplished by Christ who is 'the source of eternal salvation to all who obey him' (Heb. 5:9). Although the definite article has to be supplied, it *has* to be supplied. The writer was plainly referring to Christ as the one, the only one, who saves: he is '*the* source of eternal salvation'. All is in keeping, of course, with Christ's own assertion (John 14:6), later preached by Peter (Acts 4:12). Christ, 'securing an eternal redemption' for his people by his propitiating sacrifice – 'by means of his own blood' (Heb. 9:12) – 'having been offered once to bear the sins of many, will appear a second time, not to deal with sin but to save those who are eagerly waiting for him' (Heb. 9:28), and thus bring in their everlasting bliss.[2] In saying this, the writer indicated that one of the main ways in which he would accomplish his purpose of holding these Jewish believers to the new covenant was to set out a full exposition of salvation.

Even the briefest of skims through the book makes it evident that for the writer of Hebrews the 'great salvation' embraces far, far more than justification; at the very least, it also embraces progressive sanctification and glorification. And do not miss my 'at the very least'. When he was speaking of 'salvation', the writer spread his net to the fullest extent to include salvation's announcement in the preaching of Christ (Heb. 1:1-4) – later completed by apostolic revelation (Heb. 2:3) – its accomplishment by the sacrificial death of Christ (Heb. 1:3; 2:9-10,14-17; 9:12-28; 10:12-14; 13:12) to deliver his people from slavery (Heb. 2:16), his maintenance of them in this state of salvation by his endless, constant, peerless, effective

---

[2] See my *Undervalued*.

intercession on their behalf (Heb. 6:17-20; 7:23-28; 8:1-2; 9:24), the sanctification of believers (Heb. 2:11; 6:1-12; 9:14; 10:10,14; 13:12), their perseverance (Heb. 1:14; 2:1-4,18; 3:6; 4:1-16), and Christ's glorious return (Heb. 9:28), all of which – and more – is incorporated in the 'new order' (Heb. 9:10) – that is, the better, superior, new covenant which has superseded the inferior old covenant (Heb. 7:18-28; 8:6-13; 10:1-18). Let me stress the obvious: these things are not disjointed, isolated packets standing on a supermarket shelf calmly awaiting selection by the finicky customer; they obviously overlap and interplay with each other. They are interlocking. You cannot have one without all the rest. Indeed, in a very real sense, that is the fundamental point I am making. 'Salvation' encompasses all aspects of redemption, every part of it, all linked in an indissoluble bond, beginning with God's electing decree and leading inevitably to the saint's glorification in Christ's kingdom at the resurrection (Rom. 8:28 – 11:36). And all is combined into the new covenant which – unlike the old covenant which was temporary[3] – is the fixed, permanent, unchanging and unchangeable covenant in Christ.

No wonder, then, that the writer of Hebrews would not allow his readers even to think of going back to the superseded, old covenant. Similarly, Hebrews enforces Paul's vehemence against the *pseudadelphoi* for their efforts to contaminate the new covenant by the old. Both writers, blessed with a clearness of vision, saw the writing on the wall. And it was just one word which stared them in the face: 'DISASTER!'

We must never skip the warning passages by which the writer of Hebrews applies the new covenant. Application was key to him, and so it must be for us.[4] So serious and searching are these warnings in Hebrews, it is not unknown for commentators to gloss them so as to avoid their clear – but painful – implication.

---

[3] See my *Three Verses*.
[4] As William Perkins, the arch-Puritan preacher, said to all preachers: 'What's the use of it?' Setting out doctrine, good; applying that doctrine, better. Better? No! Best of all, essential.

What a cheap, grievous way to treat the writer's effort to maintain the glory of Christ in the new covenant! These warnings, of course, have an obvious application for unbelievers, but – and we must never allow ourselves to forget it – the writer issued them in the first instance to believers, and for believers. And one way of looking at their thrust is this: Christ has established the new covenant, rendering the old obsolete. He has brought in his own, new law. So, in terms of the wineskins, don't go back to the obsolete, worn out, tired, old leather. The consequences of getting this wrong are not to be played with. So said the writer to the Hebrews.

The writer had hardly got out of the starting blocks before he sounded his first warning note:

> Therefore we must pay much closer attention to what we have heard, lest we drift away from it. For since the message declared by angels proved to be reliable, and every transgression or disobedience received a just retribution, how shall we escape if we neglect such a great salvation? (Heb. 2:1-3).

This is patent: if the old-covenant warnings were so serious, how much more so must be the warnings of the new?

Even with the passage of 2000 years, we can still feel the passion pounding in his heart; it leaps off the page across those two millennia: the writer was not in the Senior Common Room of the local theological seminary, holding a sedate, refined debate, discussing, in a detached way, some nice, abstruse, esoteric theoretical issue over a cup of coffee. Oh no! He was engaged in a spiritual battle, a life-and-death battle, a battle he had to win. He was fighting for the souls of men.

As he had begun, so he continued:

> We are [God's] house, if indeed we hold fast our confidence and our boasting in our hope. Therefore, as the Holy Spirit says: 'Today, if you hear his voice, do not harden your hearts as [the Jews did] in the rebellion, on the day of testing in the wilderness, where your fathers put me to the test and saw my works for forty years. Therefore I was provoked with that

generation, and said: "They always go astray in their heart; they have not known my ways". As I swore in my wrath: "They shall not enter my rest"'.

Take care, brothers, lest there be in any of you an evil, unbelieving heart, leading you to fall away from the living God. But exhort one another every day, as long as it is called 'today', that none of you may be hardened by the deceitfulness of sin. For we have come to share in Christ, if indeed we hold our original confidence firm to the end (Heb. 3:6-14).

Therefore, while the promise of entering his rest still stands, let us fear lest any of you should seem to have failed to reach it (Heb. 4:1).

Let us therefore strive to enter that rest, so that no one may fall by the same sort of disobedience [as the Jews displayed in the wilderness]. For the word of God is living and active, sharper than any two-edged sword, piercing to the division of soul and of spirit, of joints and of marrow, and discerning the thoughts and intentions of the heart. And no creature is hidden from his sight, but all are naked and exposed to the eyes of him to whom we must give account. Since then we have a great high priest who has passed through the heavens, Jesus, the Son of God, let us hold fast our confession (Heb. 4:11-14).

This 'rest' must not be confined to justification, done and dusted. Nor to the intermediate state.[5] Nor to eternal glory. The use of 'strive' in 'strive to enter that rest' and 'to him to whom we must give account' proves that we have moved on from justification to include progressive sanctification and perseverance, *even to the day of judgment.*

The writer pressed on with his argument, the bit now firmly between his teeth:

It is impossible, in the case of those who have once been enlightened, who have tasted the heavenly gift, and have shared in the Holy Spirit, and have tasted the goodness of the word of God and the powers of the age to come, and then have fallen away, to restore them again to repentance, since they are crucifying once again the Son of God to their own harm and holding him up to contempt (Heb. 6:4-6).

---

[5] See my *Undervalued.*

And then we get this, clearly speaking of progressive sanctification, the living out of the justification wrought for the elect by God, and, once again, with an eye to the judgment day:

> Therefore, brothers, since we have confidence to enter the holy places by the blood of Jesus, by the new and living way that he opened for us through the curtain, that is, through his flesh, and since we have a great priest over the house of God, let us draw near with a true heart in full assurance of faith, with our hearts sprinkled clean from an evil conscience and our bodies washed with pure water. Let us hold fast the confession of our hope without wavering, for he who promised is faithful. And let us consider how to stir up one another to love and good works, not neglecting to meet together, as is the habit of some, but encouraging one another, and all the more as you see the Day drawing near.
>
> For if we go on sinning deliberately after receiving the knowledge of the truth, there no longer remains a sacrifice for sins, but a fearful expectation of judgment, and a fury of fire that will consume the adversaries. Anyone who has set aside the law of Moses dies without mercy on the evidence of two or three witnesses. How much worse punishment, do you think, will be deserved by the one who has trampled underfoot the Son of God, and has profaned the blood of the covenant by which he was sanctified, and has outraged the Spirit of grace? For we know him who said: 'Vengeance is mine; I will repay'. And again: 'The Lord will judge his people'. It is a fearful thing to fall into the hands of the living God (Heb. 10:19-31).

The writer was in full flow:

> You joyfully accepted the plundering of your property, since you knew that you yourselves had a better possession and an abiding one. Therefore do not throw away your confidence, which has a great reward. For you have need of endurance, so that when you have done the will of God you may receive what is promised. For: 'Yet a little while, and the coming one will come and will not delay; but my righteous one shall live by faith, and if he shrinks back, my soul has no pleasure in him'. But we are not of those who shrink back and are destroyed, but of those who have faith and preserve their souls (Heb. 10:34-39).

Wise teacher that he was, the writer then (in Hebrews 11) reminded his readers (ex Jews, remember) of the heroic saga they all knew so well, the long history of countless men and women of faith who had lived and died in the days before the coming of the Messiah and the new covenant. Nobody could miss what he was saying. Yes, these men and women were men and women of faith, but for each and every one of them, their faith was shown in a lifetime of works and obedience. There was no exception. In a new-covenant sense, their justification by faith, in every case, was demonstrated by a life of works done in faith; in short, their justification inevitably led to their progressive sanctification and perseverance. If the writer – who said this:

> ...You have become dull of hearing. For though by this time you ought to be teachers, you need someone to teach you again the basic principles of the oracles of God. You need milk, not solid food, for everyone who lives on milk is unskilled in the word of righteousness, since he is a child. But solid food is for the mature, for those who have their powers of discernment trained by constant practice to distinguish good from evil (Heb. 5:11-14)...

...had lived until the twentieth century, he would never have allowed cheap talk about 'once saved, always saved', or: 'I'm only a carnal Christian'.[6] For him, progressive sanctification and perseverance was as vital as justification. No works? No justification!

He resolutely pressed home the obvious application:

---

[6] An excuse offered by those who try to justify their talk of Christ being their Saviour but not their Lord. In other words, they turn Paul's rebuke of the Corinthians on its head to make it a compliment, an explanation, a justification! 'I, brothers, could not address you as spiritual people, but as people of the flesh, as infants in Christ. I fed you with milk, not solid food, for you were not ready for it. And even now you are not yet ready, for you are still of the flesh. For while there is jealousy and strife among you, are you not of the flesh and behaving only in a human way? For when one says: "I follow Paul," and another: "I follow Apollos", are you not being merely human?' (1 Cor. 3:1-4). 'Flesh' and 'spirit', once again.

Therefore, since we are surrounded by so great a cloud of witnesses [the testimony of the believers listed in Hebrews 11], let us also lay aside every weight, and sin which clings so closely, and let us run with endurance the race that is set before us, looking to Jesus, the founder and perfecter of our faith, who for the joy that was set before him endured the cross, despising the shame, and is seated at the right hand of the throne of God (Heb. 12:1-2).

And that 'cloud of witnesses', remember, lived in the days of the old covenant, before the Spirit had been poured out![7] The implication is clear: a better covenant enables – and demands – a better devotion. Above all:

Consider [Christ] who endured from sinners such hostility against himself, so that you may not grow weary or fainthearted. In your struggle against sin you have not yet resisted to the point of shedding your blood. And have you forgotten the exhortation that addresses you as sons? 'My son, do not regard lightly the discipline of the Lord, nor be weary when reproved by him. For the Lord disciplines the one he loves, and chastises every son whom he receives'.

It is for discipline that you have to endure. God is treating you as sons. For what son is there whom his father does not discipline? If you are left without discipline, in which all have participated, then you are illegitimate children and not sons. Besides this, we have had earthly fathers who disciplined us and we respected them. Shall we not much more be subject to the Father of spirits and live? For they disciplined us for a short time as it seemed best to them, but he disciplines us for our good, that we may share his holiness. For the moment all discipline seems painful rather than pleasant, but later it yields the peaceful fruit of righteousness to those who have been trained by it.

Therefore lift your drooping hands and strengthen your weak knees, and make straight paths for your feet, so that what is

---

[7] 'Whoever believes in me, as the Scripture has said: "Out of his heart will flow rivers of living water". Now this he said about the Spirit, whom those who believed in him were to receive, for as yet the Spirit had not been given, because Jesus was not yet glorified' (John 7:38-39). The new covenant might well be described as the age of the Spirit (Luke 24:46-49; Acts 1:5,8; 2:1-4; 4:31; Gal. 5:16-25, and so on).

lame may not be put out of joint but rather be healed. Strive for peace with everyone, and for the holiness without which no one will see the Lord. See to it that no one fails to obtain the grace of God; that no 'root of bitterness' springs up and causes trouble, and by it many become defiled; that no one is sexually immoral or unholy like Esau, who sold his birthright for a single meal. For you know that afterward, when he desired to inherit the blessing, he was rejected, for he found no chance to repent, though he sought it with tears (Heb. 12:3-17).[8]

Believers are not under the old covenant and its law. No! They are in Christ, under his law. As the Hebrews writer put it to his readers: You are no longer living in the shadow of Sinai (Heb. 12:18-21):

...But you have come to Mount Zion and to the city of the living God, the heavenly Jerusalem, and to innumerable angels in festal gathering, and to the assembly of the firstborn who are enrolled in heaven, and to God, the judge of all, and to the spirits of the righteous made perfect, and to Jesus, the Mediator of a new covenant, and to the sprinkled blood that speaks a better word than the blood of Abel (Heb. 12:22-24).

Consequently:

See that you do not refuse him who is speaking. For if they did not escape when they refused him who warned them on earth, much less will we escape if we reject him who warns from heaven... Therefore let us be grateful for receiving a kingdom that cannot be shaken, and thus let us offer to God acceptable worship, with reverence and awe, for our God is a consuming fire (Heb. 12:25-29).

All this change, the fulfilling of the old covenant, the bringing in of the new, came only at tremendous cost to Christ, a cost believers must never let slip from their minds:

Jesus also suffered outside the gate in order to sanctify the people through his own blood. Therefore let us go to him outside the camp and bear the reproach he endured. For here we have no lasting city, but we seek the city that is to come. Through him then let us continually offer up a sacrifice of

---

[8] That is, he couldn't change his choice.

praise to God, that is, the fruit of lips that acknowledge his name. Do not neglect to do good and to share what you have, for such sacrifices are pleasing to God (Heb. 13:12-16).

In particular, Hebrews addresses progressive sanctification. It is clear that the writer could never for a moment have contemplated that anybody could dream of treating justification and progressive sanctification as separate entities:

Therefore, holy brothers, you who share in a heavenly calling, consider Jesus, the apostle and high priest of our confession, who was faithful to him who appointed him, just as Moses also was faithful in all God's house. For Jesus has been counted worthy of more glory than Moses... We are his house, if [and, I might add, only if – DG] indeed[9] we hold fast our confidence and our boasting in our hope... Take care, brothers, lest there be in any of you an evil, unbelieving heart, leading you to fall away from the living God. But exhort one another every day, as long as it is called 'today', that none of you may be hardened by the deceitfulness of sin. For we have come to share in Christ, if indeed we hold our original confidence firm to the end... Therefore, while the promise of entering his rest still stands, let us fear lest any of you should seem to have failed to reach it... Let us therefore strive to enter that rest, so that no one may fall by the same sort of disobedience. For the word of God is living and active, sharper than any two-edged sword, piercing to the division of soul and of spirit, of joints and of marrow, and discerning the thoughts and intentions of the heart. And no creature is hidden from his sight, but all are naked and exposed to the eyes of him to whom we must give account.
Since then we have a great high priest who has passed through the heavens, Jesus, the Son of God, let us hold fast our confession. For we do not have a high priest who is unable to sympathise with our weaknesses, but one who in every respect has been tempted as we are, yet without sin. Let us then with confidence draw near to the throne of grace, that we may receive mercy and find grace to help in time of need (Heb. 3:1 – 4:16).

His virtually closing remarks put the icing on his cake:

---

[9] The 'indeed' surely makes the point I added in my parenthesis.

Now may the God of peace who brought again from the dead our Lord Jesus, the great shepherd of the sheep, by the blood of the eternal covenant, equip you with everything good that you may do his will, working in us that which is pleasing in his sight, through Jesus Christ, to whom be glory forever and ever. Amen (Heb. 13:20-21).

Just before I close this article, let me, at the risk of boring you by repetition, make my purpose as clear as I can. I am anxious to press home the point that 'salvation' is far more than justification. In particular, 'salvation' includes progressive sanctification, leading to glorification. It is vital to grasp this principle and not let it go – not least when reading the closing chapters of my *False Bothers*. I wrote that book about the way Paul dealt with the *pseudadelphoi* not as an academic study of a historical spat, but as enforcing a biblical principle which we need to understand and apply today. And in that important task of contemporary application, nothing could be more necessary than to make sure we allow no daylight whatsoever between justification and progressive sanctification leading to glorification. That has been what this article has been about.

Let me illustrate what I am saying by an episode (or two episodes in one) drawn from the old covenant. We know that Israel was delivered from Egypt by means of the Passover:

The LORD said to Moses and Aaron in the land of Egypt: 'This month shall be for you the beginning of months. It shall be the first month of the year for you. Tell all the congregation of Israel that on the tenth day of this month every man shall take a lamb according to their fathers' houses, a lamb for a household... You shall keep it until the fourteenth day of this month, when the whole assembly of the congregation of Israel shall kill their lambs at twilight. Then they shall take some of the blood and put it on the two doorposts and the lintel of the houses in which they eat it... It is the LORD's Passover' (Ex. 12:1-11).

The spiritual equivalent in the new covenant is obvious: it is the elect sinner's deliverance from sin, death and slavery by the sacrificial, atoning work of Christ, the imputation of the merits of his blood and righteousness to all who believe:

Christ, our Passover lamb, has been sacrificed [for us] (1 Cor. 5:7).

You were ransomed from the futile ways inherited from your forefathers, not with perishable things such as silver or gold, but with the precious blood of Christ, like that of a lamb without blemish or spot (1 Pet. 1:18-19).

For our [that is, believers'] sake he [that is, the Father] made him [that is, the Son] to be sin who knew no sin, so that in him we might become the righteousness of God (2 Cor. 5:21).

Christ was crucified on the Feast of Passover:

On the first day of Unleavened Bread, when they sacrificed the Passover lamb, his disciples said to him: 'Where will you have us go and prepare for you to eat the Passover?'... And when they had sung a hymn, they went out to the Mount of Olives... And they led Jesus to the high priest. And all the chief priests and the elders and the scribes came together... Pilate, wishing to satisfy the crowd, released for them Barabbas, and having scourged Jesus, he delivered him to be crucified (Mark 14:12,26,53; 15:15).

Now it was the day of Preparation of the Passover. It was about the sixth hour [Pilate] said to the Jews: 'Behold your King!' They cried out: 'Away with him, away with him, crucify him!' Pilate said to them, "Shall I crucify your King?' The chief priests answered: 'We have no king but Caesar'. So he delivered him over to them to be crucified (John 19:14-16).

We know that Israel's deliverance from Egypt was with the intention of settling them in the land God had promised to Abraham. We also know that Israel initially failed in this (Numbers 13 & 14). But, after a generation of judgment in the wilderness, Israel, once again, came to Canaan, and this time they were obedient and successful (Joshua 1 – 5). In accordance with God's command, Israel set up twelve stones drawn from the bed of the Jordan to commemorate the miracle:

The people came up out of the Jordan on the tenth day of the first month, and they encamped at Gilgal on the east border of Jericho. And [the] twelve stones, which [at God's command (Josh. 4:1-7)] they took out of the Jordan, Joshua set up at Gilgal. And he said to the people of Israel: 'When your children ask their fathers in times to come: 'What do these stones mean?' then you shall let your children know, 'Israel passed over this Jordan on dry ground'. For the LORD your God dried up the waters of the Jordan for you until you passed over, as the LORD your God did to the Red Sea, which he dried up for us until we passed over, so that all the peoples of the earth may know that the hand of the LORD is mighty, that you may fear the LORD your God forever' (Josh. 4:19-24).

Scripture draws special attention to the date:

While the people of Israel were encamped at Gilgal, they kept the Passover on the fourteenth day of the month in the evening on the plains of Jericho (Josh. 5:10).

The coincidence of dates of the Passover and the crossing of the Jordan, and their memorials, is no accident. I use the term strictly – that is, co-incidence:

With a strong hand the LORD has brought you out of Egypt... When the LORD brings you into the land of the Canaanites, as he swore to you and your fathers, and shall give it to you... (Ex. 13:9-11).

Clearly, God was teaching the Israelites – and us today – an important spiritual truth.[10] While it goes without saying that Israel could not leave Egypt and enter Canaan in one physical act on the same day, even so, spiritually speaking, Israel's leaving Egypt and entering Canaan was one. Whatever Canaan is taken to typify – the believer's present rest in Christ, or his eternal bliss – the new-covenant meaning and fulfilment of the old-covenant shadow of the dates and memorials is patent. 'Salvation' is one event, one happening: from election to glorification, 'salvation' is one; it must not be chopped into bits, and treated as free-standing, independent, isolated entities. In particular, we must constantly keep justification and progressive sanctification in one intimate, unbroken union with each other.[11] That is my point. Can a sinner be justified but show no evidence

---

[10] Any who think I make too much of it should read Num. 14:34.

[11] For more on this, see my 'Memorials 1' and my 'Memorials 2' on my sermonaudio.com page.

of progressive sanctification? Of course not. And surely nobody would suggest that progressive sanctification is possible without justification!

# *Ignored Intelligence: The Cost*

Market Garden.

No! Rid yourself of all nice thoughts of an idyllic thatched cottage, roses twining round the door, rows and rows of lettuces, spring greens or runner beans in the field. Think, rather, Second World War, September 1944, Belgian/Dutch border, and Highway 69 from Leopoldville to Arnhem.

Operation Market Garden.

Field-Marshal Bernard Montgomery's plan was in two parts: Market and Garden. Market would capture (intact) the various bridges along the road (remember, Holland is a land of waterways, dykes, canals and rivers) by the largest-ever (until then) drop of paratroops (American, British and Polish), in order to keep the only road open for Garden, an assault by the British army up the road. The immediate object was to take and secure the vital, massive Arnhem bridge over the Rhine, to enable, in the ultimate, Allied ground forces to pour into the Ruhr, thus producing an early German collapse, and so 'bringing the boys home by Christmas'.

There were some successes, but as a whole the operation was a failure. In a personal sense – in particular, for the civilian citizens of Arnhem, and especially for the British and Polish paratroops spearheading the attack at Arnhem, and the Americans killed or injured taking the intermediate bridges, and for the hapless Dutch trapped in their subsequent prolonged subjection under the Nazis leading to many thousands of deaths, and the long, slogging-battle throughout the winter that followed the fiasco – it was a catastrophe of the first magnitude.

Why?

I am not a military historian, and this is not intended to be an article for military buffs, but when all the reasons – and excuses – are weighed – the intransigence, arrogance, over-confidence and impatience of the planners, fuelled by the mutual loathing of Bernard Montgomery and George Patton, fog in England, the breakdown in communications, poor tactics, the marshy terrain, the accidents of war, the clogging mass of jubilant citizens freed from years of jackboot tyranny, and so on – Market Garden was a disaster *even before it started.*[1]

In saying this, I intend no slur whatsoever on the courage, heroism and grievous, indescribable suffering of the troops on the ground: the rank and file involved deserve nothing but praise. The Americans (with increasing difficulty) succeeded in capturing the lower bridges, not all, alas, intact. But it was at Arnhem where the failure was fatally evident. And, remember, Arnhem was key. Again, this is to cast no slur on the British (joined later by Polish) paratroops who formed the spearhead of the operation at Arnhem. Criticism must be directed much higher up the chain, much higher.

How high?

The very top, including Dwight Eisenhower and, especially, Bernard Montgomery.

Why?

It was not a failure, as was so often said – and is still being said – because of a lack of intelligence. Almost the exact opposite is the case. Intelligence there was in plenty; the failure came about because the top planners chose to ignore the facts. Early writers of the history of the operation, perhaps, had an excuse for not apportioning blame where it truly belongs. Those writers laboured under a grievous disability: they were simply unaware of – or, at least, were only dimly aware of – Operation Ultra.

---

[1] For the military aspects of this article, I have relied on Joel J.Jeffson: 'Operation Market-Garden: Ultra Intelligence Ignored', a thesis presented to the Faculty of the US Army Command and General Staff College, Fort Leavenworth, Kansas, 2002; Ronald Lewin: *Ultra Goes To War: The Secret Story*, Penguin Books, London, 1978, pp346-351,355,357; Wikipedia.

Operation Ultra was the top, top-secret organisation at Bletchley Park which was established to crack German codes and so supply the Allies with high-grade intelligence. This secrecy was successfully maintained for years, even after the war. It was initially relaxed in 1978, and even more so in 1989. As Adrienne Wilmoth Lerner reports:

> The veil of secrecy extended to the wartime staff of Bletchley Park, none of whom disclosed information about Ultra until the project was officially declassified in 1989.[2]

But now that this secrecy has, to a large measure, been relaxed, we know the real reason for the disaster at Arnhem. When all the other reasons and excuses are factored in, the truth is *Operation Market Garden was absolutely doomed before it started.* **More than that, the top brass knew it was.**

By this stage in the war, Bletchley was supplying first-class, highest-grade intelligence of the German plans. Ultra had cracked the German codes, and were translating German radio traffic so that all who were in the know at the Allied uppermost level of Market Garden were being supplied with a stream of up-to-date intelligence of the enemy, his dispositions, and his plans. Ultra was not faultless in this complicated affair – an early, vital decrypt was passed on with slightly lower grading of importance than it deserved. But, even so, the top brass planning Market Garden knew it all.

And the precise information they were receiving told them that the British and Polish paratroops would be slaughtered, and that, consequently, there was no chance whatsoever that the Arnhem bridge would be secured for a bridgehead into the Ruhr.

Why?

In mid-June, Hitler had transferred a crack SS Panzer (tank) Corps to the West, a Corps which had fought savage battles on the Eastern front. They were battle-hardened. On 4th September,

---

[2] Adrienne Wilmoth Lerner: 'Ultra, Operation', encyclopedia.com website.

Hitler put von Rundstedt in charge of the German army in northern France, Belgium and Holland, with the aim of halting the German disintegration. Rundstedt knew that the Panzers, key to his defence against the inevitable Allied onslaught, urgently needed rest and re-equipment, and for that reason he selected a quiet spot to which he could move his tanks – Arnhem. The German decision was entirely fortuitous, but Rundstedt had unwittingly put his finger on the key spot. The unavoidably lightly-armed, temporarily-supplied, British (and, later) Polish paratroops were going to be dropped virtually on top of a crack tank Corps. It was like sending men with pea-shooters, with a limited supply of peas, against a castle manned by cannon. It was going to be nothing but a rout and a slaughter, a massacre.

And the top Allied planning brass – because of Ultra transcripts – knew all this, and knew it down to the finest detail. And knew it in good time.

And as if this was not enough, Dutch resistance intelligence independently confirmed aspects of all this. So much so, air reconnaissance took photographs to verify it all, clearly showing camouflaged German tanks in the vital area.

All this extremely high-grade intelligence was dismissed out of hand by the powers-that-be. Major Brian Urquhart, Air Intelligence, who warned I British Airborne Corps commander, Lieutenant-General Frederick Browning, was waved away as hysterical, and ordered on sick leave. Even higher up the chain, Major-General Sir Kenneth Strong, Eisenhower's Chief Intelligence Officer, took the evidence to the Chief of Staff at headquarters, Bedell Smith, and the latter warned Montgomery. 'I got nowhere', Smith recorded. 'Montgomery simply waived my objections airily aside'.

Not a scrap of all this essential intelligence was passed down the line to the lower commanders, nor the men, who under them, would have to face the tanks – tanks – with nothing but light arms, facing overwhelming armour while short of ammunition, food and medical supplies. (The Germans held the pre-arranged dropping zones for supplies. None, therefore, reached the stranded British. The Germans got it all). The British paratroops were entirely ignorant of what was waiting for them. (The Poles were going to be detained in England by fog). Of course, the Germans, too, were not fully aware of what was coming, and they made their mistakes, but as soon as they woke up to what was happening on the ground, it was just a question of time. US losses were nearly 4000; British and Polish (those who had to face the Panzers) about 12000.

Joel Jeffson began the conclusion to his thesis:

> Operation Market Garden did not fail as the result of a major intelligence error, as stated by numerous authors. Information was available that clearly showed that the German situation in Holland changed dramatically from 4th September to 17th September. While the intelligence community, as a whole, was slow to respond to this change, it nevertheless did. Their warnings though came after the decision to execute the operation had already been made, and the senior commanders were unwilling to cancel the operation. Ultra, the tool that helped Montgomery succeed in Africa, was regrettably set aside in Holland. The intercepts that told the Allies that panzer divisions were relocating to the vicinity of the planned drop zones and airborne objectives were discounted within Montgomery's 21st Army Group, and this information was not passed down to the combat units that were tasked to execute the operation. Even the commander of the British XXX Corps later said: 'I had no idea whatever that the 9th and 10th Panzer Divisions were refitting just north-east of Arnhem'.[3]

* * *

I have said this is not an article for military buffs. So... who is it for? And why have I re-told this tragic saga?

Because it contains invaluable lessons – lessons far beyond military operations. It is altogether too easy for us to have first-class warnings about some impending disaster, and yet ignore them and press on regardless. It might be for reasons of

---

[3] Jeffson p80.

arrogance, over-confidence, or whatever, but ignoring clear warnings carries a big price tag. But not, as in Market Garden, for others, the men on the ground, at the sharp end of the battle, *but for ourselves.*

I am speaking spiritually. Don't switch off! We ignore spiritual warnings, spiritual intelligence, at our peril, *our **own** peril.*

God has warned us all:

> [God] commands all people everywhere to repent, because he has fixed a day on which he will judge the world in righteousness by a man whom he has appointed [that is, Christ]; and of this he has given assurance to all by raising him from the dead (Acts 17:30-31).

> God so loved the world, that he gave his only begotten Son, that whoever believes in him should not perish but have eternal life. For God did not send his Son into the world to condemn the world, but in order that the world might be saved through him. Whoever believes in him is not condemned, but whoever does not believe is condemned already, because he has not believed in the name of the only begotten Son of God... Whoever believes in the Son has eternal life; whoever does not obey the Son shall not see life, but the wrath of God remains on him (John 3:16-18,36).

Paul was a preacher who warned all his readers and hearers (Acts 20:31; 1 Cor. 4:14; Col. 1:28; 1 Thess. 5:14). So was Ezekiel (Ezek. 3:17-21; 33:3-9). And that is what I am doing here. Reader, I am warning you.

The psalmist was warned of God, so was Cornelius, and so was Noah, and they all three were glad of the warning and acted on it. They did not shrug their shoulders and move on (Ps. 19:11; Acts 10:22; Heb. 11:7).

Alas, I feel like Jeremiah, and have to speak as he did:

> Hear this, O foolish and senseless people, who have eyes, but see not, who have ears, but hear not (Jer. 5:21).

> To whom shall I speak and give warning, that they may hear? Behold, their ears are closed, they cannot listen; behold, the

word of the LORD is to them an object of scorn; they take no pleasure in it (Jer. 6:10).

'Walk in all the way that I command you, that it may be well with you'. But they did not obey or incline their ear, but walked in their own counsels and the stubbornness of their evil hearts, and went backward and not forward. From the day that your fathers came out of the land of Egypt to this day, I have persistently sent all my servants the prophets to them, day after day. Yet they did not listen to me or incline their ear, but stiffened their neck. They did worse than their fathers. So you shall speak all these words to them, but they will not listen to you. You shall call to them, but they will not answer you. And you shall say to them: 'This is the nation that did not obey the voice of the LORD their God, and did not accept discipline; truth has perished; it is cut off from their lips' (Jer. 7:23-28).

\* \* \*

Let me bring this to a close with two episodes which highlight the choice I am putting before you.

First, Abimelech, a king of Gerar (Gen. 20:7-18). He was warned of God. He heard that warning. He heeded that warning, and acted accordingly. And God spared him.

Secondly, the prospective sons-in-law of Lot (Gen. 19:14). Lot warned them of impending disaster. They treated it as a joke. They perished in the succeeding destruction.

Which of the two are you?

# The Case of the Curious Blind Spot:
# John Jewel – Model Reformer?

On the 17th November 1558, a battered barque, its yards hanging forlorn from its three-masted spars, its rigging torn to shreds and flapping in the (thank God!) now-easing wind, creaked its way slowly free of the storm clouds into what the young master – actually, the young mistress – hoped would prove to be calmer waters and fairer weather. It seemed so. A watery sun was peering through the cloud. For the moment. But that ship's mistress, though young, was not going to let herself be lulled into premature relaxation. She knew, by years of bitter, personal experience that appearances can be deceiving, very deceiving. The gale had eased, and the waves subsided – at least for a time – yes, but these waters were notoriously treacherous; uncharted, hidden shoals lurked ahead; pirates – Spanish raiders in particular – could attack at any moment. The broken vessel had not yet reached safety; there seemed no end to the threats which could take it beneath the waves before it could, at last, wearily drop anchor in the shelter of a safe haven.

I am, of course, talking about the creaking barque called England, the death of Mary – the Mary of Bloody infamy – and the accession of Elizabeth I.

Elizabeth was the undoubted Queen of England. Over that, there was no real dispute – except, of course, there was always her cousin, Mary, Queen of Scots, dangerously waiting in the wings. For the moment, however, she was relatively safe. But Elizabeth's first twenty-five years had been an anxious existence fraught with danger on every hand; the life of the daughter of Henry VIII and Anne Boleyn had hung on a thread ever since she had first seen the light of day in 1533. Her father had had her mother beheaded when she was only a two-year-old toddler, and England, during her short lifetime, had been hurtled through a time of unparalleled political-religious upheaval. The

State Church – and in those days, that meant the State itself, for the two formed one Commonwealth – had been on a roller-coaster. It had been switched from centuries of Roman popery into the short-lived, self-appointed popery of her father, Henry VIII. There followed a brief lurch Geneva-ward under the reforming reign of her half-brother, the teenage consumptive, Edward VI. Then it plunged into near-civil-war, brought about by the hare-brained scheme to avert a swing back to Rome by capturing the throne for the young Lady Jane Grey, installing – using – her in their dangerous game as an unwilling (to start with) pawn (a pawn who would lose her head within a few months). Then came a violent – literally, burning – hard-nosed return to a rabid, fully-Romanised popery under Elizabeth's older half-sister, Mary, who, by her marriage to the Spanish king, Philip II, had potentially brought England under the domination of the most powerful papist kingdom in the world.[1] Phew! Listing it takes one's breath away. What it must have been for the vulnerable Elizabeth living her precarious youthful years through such sweeping changes defies description.

One thing had remained a constant throughout all these turbulent years, however. The State Church might have had its

---

[1] Catherine of Aragon, the discarded wife of Henry VIII, had wreaked her revenge by rearing her daughter Mary as a bitter, rabid Roman Catholic, one who, in time, she hoped, might reinstate Romanism in England. Because of Henry's carnal shenanigans, coupled with the all-consuming necessity to produce a male heir to avoid the catastrophe of the Wars of the Roses, Elizabeth's mother, Anne, had, as already noted, been beheaded when Elizabeth was only two, and the child declared illegitimate. During the years of Mary's savage, brutal, repression of Protestants, Elizabeth had been imprisoned for nearly a year on suspicion of support for Protestants. In the eyes of Mary, Elizabeth could easily have become the natural focus of rebellion, even revolution, to depose Mary and produce a Protestant State. Elizabeth's death was the only sure insurance against it. Fortunately for Elizabeth, she was never led to the block. (This was played out in reverse when Elizabeth had Mary Queen of Scots in her power. Faced with a possible invasion by Philip II, William Cecil baited a trap into which Mary naively fell, and she was executed in 1587 at Fotheringay Castle).

beliefs and practices abruptly and violently changed for it by the will of the Monarch – whether Henry, Edward or Mary – or by the various political and religious schemers pulling the strings behind the throne, but every English man, woman and child, whether high-born or low, rich or poor, had had to recognise and attend that State Church, whatever its official beliefs and practices, owning the Sovereign as Supreme Governor (whatever views that Sovereign held) in all matters of religion. Conformity was essential; conformity at all costs. Deviants – heretics in the eyes of the State – had been given short shrift. Fines, prison, the gallows, the block or the stake awaited, and they were not idle measures. The axe was sharp. Keep your head down – or you might lose it! Add politics to the mix, the politics of royal succession, international politics, the politics of alliances and war, the politics of those lurking in the shadows just behind the throne... oh yes, the times had been dangerous, dangerous in the extreme. And for none more so than that young Princess – or was she merely the Lady? – now come to the throne – Elizabeth I. Thus, on the 17th November 1558, Elizabeth emerged from her years of anxious existence under constant threat from all sides to become the (virtually) undisputed Queen of England. All danger had not passed, however. In addition to the above, the Pope would soon (in 1570) declare her a heretic and excommunicate her. At a stroke, Elizabeth's life (as well as her eternity – in the eyes of Rome) was at stake, with every Romanist turned into a potential traitor, licensed to kill the Queen.

Although she was not herself deeply religiously-committed, Elizabeth was sympathetic to Roman Catholicism. Nevertheless, her overriding religious policy as Monarch and Supreme Governor of the Church of England would be simple and clear-cut, and to that she would be resolutely committed throughout her long reign: uniformity in all her realm, uniformity at all costs, one religion, and that religion to be moderate, stemming neither from Rome or Geneva, though heavily tinged with the former.

But this inevitably meant opposition, opposition from two wings – Papists, on the one wing, who hoped for a return to Rome, and, on the other wing, opposition from those who would become known as Puritans, men and women who grudgingly accepted the present state of things while hoping for a more thorough-going Geneva-ward reform. Some Romanists – recusants – would not conform, and paid the price. But, in the main, the Papists would outwardly conform. For all of them, their papistry was maintained – and advanced – by a secret, hidden, underground priesthood, especially and increasingly of a Jesuit order, illegally trained in English seminaries on the Continent, and smuggled back into England. The Puritans would give a niggardly conformity, but, for a while, become more and more vocal and practical in their demands for reform. A relatively small number of them had spent time on the Continent during Mary's reign, and when they returned to England under Elizabeth, many of them were hoping to put into practice what they had learnt of Reformed Churches in Zurich, Strasbourg, Geneva, and such places, looking in short for further Geneva-ward reformation of the English State Church. As for the general population and the lower clergy, it is probably fair to say that although the majority had a liking for the old, familiar, showy Catholicism, the vicar of Bray had fathered many sons and daughters.[2] Outward conformity was all that would be asked; consequently, outwardly the people would conform. But as for what was going through their minds and hearts – if anything – was another question. Elizabeth wisely said she would not make a window into men's souls (an impossibility, in any case!); as long as the people were willing to conform outwardly to the State Church, to attend its services for at least

---

[2] Thomas Fuller: 'The vivacious vicar [of Bray] living under King Henry VIII, King Edward VI, Queen Mary, and Queen Elizabeth, was first a Papist, then a Protestant, then a Papist, then a Protestant again. He had seen some martyrs burnt... and found this fire too hot for his tender temper. This vicar, being taxed [attacked] by one for being a turncoat and an inconstant changeling, said: "Not so, for I always kept my principle, which is this – to live and die the vicar of Bray"' (Thomas Fuller: Worthies of England, 1662).

the minimum number of times demanded each year, be married and have their children christened under its rites, and kept their noses clean – holding their ideas and beliefs to themselves, avoiding open criticism of the Elizabethan Settlement – they could believe what they liked. Or nothing.[3]

\* \* \*

Enter John Jewel (24th May 1522 – 23rd September 1571). Jewel had been among those who fled to the Continent during the reign of Mary, even though he was far from being one with most of the other Marian exiles. Upon Elizabeth's succession, he returned to England, became heavily committed to supporting the Elizabethan Settlement, being installed as Bishop of Salisbury in 1560. Although in his youth he had compromised with Rome, he had publicly repented to become staunchly anti-Roman. He adopted an even stronger stance against the Puritans. Indeed, in his final sermon, Jewel strongly argued against the Puritan faction, describing them as worse than the Roman Catholics. It is recorded that under his reign as bishop, Wiltshire was 'singularly free of trouble-makers, Romanist and Puritan alike'. Archbishop Richard Bancroft, the arch-enemy of the Puritans, had Jewel's works published in one volume in 1609, ordering a copy of the work to be placed in all the churches.[4] The significance of this can be measured by Edward Hyde's comment: 'If Bancroft had lived, he would

---

[3] Some of the Romanists who did conform surreptitiously (or not) read papist books during the service. Protestants could be no better. Indeed, C.H.Spurgeon, three hundred years later, could speak of 'Hodge, the hedger and ditcher, who remarked to a Christian man with whom he was talking: "I loikes Sunday, I does; I loikes Sunday". "And what makes you like Sunday?" "Cause, you see, it's a day of rest; I goes down to the old church, I gets into a pew, and puts my legs up, and I thinks o' nothin". It is to be feared that in town as well as in country this thinking of nothing is a very usual thing' (C.H.Spurgeon: 'The Uses of Anecdotes and Illustrations', *Lectures to my Students*, Vol.2).
[4] John and Angela Magee: 'Bishop John Jewel', p3, website of Emmanuel Church, Salisbury.

quickly have extinguished all that fire in England which had been kindled at Geneva'.[5]

In summary, Jewel, by preaching and print, devoted himself to defending the Elizabethan Settlement, primarily against Roman Catholics, though with even less sympathy for Puritans. In a sermon on 26th November 1559, he had challenged all comers to prove the Roman Catholic case out of the Scriptures, or the Councils or Fathers of the first six hundred years after Christ. He repeated his challenge in 1560, and a priest, Dr Henry Cole, responded. The 'Great Controversy' that followed produced over sixty polemical works, and set the tone and content of much of the subsequent debate between the Anglican Church and Roman Catholics. Jewel's main work was his *Apologia ecclesiae Anglicanae* (the Apology of the Anglican Church), published in 1562. This statement of the position of the Church of England against the Roman Catholic Church has proved fundamental to all subsequent controversy in this area. Lady Anne Bacon's 1564 translation of Jewel's book into English meant that Jewel's work reached a much wider audience, and enabled it to find its dominant role in the argument.

\* \* \*

Why am I saying all this? I am no supporter of the Elizabethan Settlement, nor of the even weaker 1660-1662 Anglian Settlement under the restored Charles II, and certainly not of the present day Church of England. Far, far from it! I tell those who are interested that I quit the Church of England in 1580.[6]

No! Anglicanism in itself doesn't interest me. Rather, I am concerned with Jewel's openness about the basis, the authority, the justification, for the Church of England, his stance against the Puritans, and the surprising way some Reformed people view him today.

---

[5] Wikipedia.
[6] See my *Battle*, and my article 'Robert Browne: Thinking the Unthinkable' on my sermonaudio.com page.

Early in his *The Apology of the Church of England*, John Jewel made his position – and the Church's position – crystal clear when he stated:

> To the intent all men may see what is our judgment of every part of [the] Christian religion, and may resolve with themselves, whether the faith which they shall see confirmed by the words of Christ, by the writings of the apostles, by the testimonies of the Catholic fathers...[7]

Let me clear up a couple of possible misunderstandings. Jewel was not writing an 'apology' in the sense of apologising, saying he was sorry. Quite the opposite! He was setting out an explanation, a justification; he was justifying the stance of the Church of England. And, although he was, in the main, justifying the Church of England against Romanism, in this extract by 'Catholic' he did not mean *Roman* Catholic. He was saying the Church of England's stance was in accord with Scripture and the writings of the Fathers; Scripture and the Fathers constituted the authority of the Church of England; its beliefs and practices were warranted by Scripture and the Fathers. That is what he was saying, and saying loud and clear.

Without any suggestion of patronisation, I commend Jewel for his honesty.

The devil, however, as always is in the detail. That 'and' ruins all. When men preach Christ 'and' for justification, the 'and' ruins all. Christ is all (Col. 3:11). When Jewel says Scripture 'and' the Fathers is the authority for the Church of England, the game is up.

What is my purpose in writing this article? Twofold.

*First*, this question of authority. Jewel's (and, consequently, the Church of England's) basis for doctrine and practice was (and remains) Scripture as understood by the Fathers. In reality, this meant – and still means – the Fathers. The Anglicans are not

---

[7] John Jewel: *The Apology of the Church of England*, Cassell, London, 1888, first published in 1562 in Latin, first translated into English by Lady Anne Bacon in 1564.

alone. Something similar can be said for the Reformed. Though they claim that Scripture is their authority, as they show by their preaching, their books and their articles, it is Scripture 'and' the favoured Confession. In fact, it is in reality Scripture as understood in light of the Confession. And, of course, the Confession – the Westminster or the 1689 Particular Baptist – depends heavily on Calvin who himself was highly influenced by the Fathers and the medieval Church.

*Secondly*, it is what I call 'The Case of the Curious Blindspot'. As I have noted, Emmanuel Church, Salisbury publishes the highly-laudatory article 'Bishop John Jewel', and the writers of this article, in their application of Jewel's life and work, make the point:

> As we remember the life and controversies of Jewel, let us consider the advance which Roman doctrine is presently making within the Protestant churches. Our zeal for pure doctrine in the church of Christ ought to be like that of Jewel and other Protestant Reformers. We are debtors to these men who have left us the foundations of Reformed principles.

'Our zeal for pure doctrine in the church of Christ ought to be like that of Jewel and other Protestant Reformers. We are debtors to these men who have left us the foundations of Reformed principles'. Really? What a remarkable statement to be found on the website of such a church as Emmanuel, which is absolutely committed to the 1689 Particular Baptist Confession of Faith, and devoted to the Puritans! Indeed, immediately under the heading 'Beliefs', the website has a copy of the famous painting of the Westminster Divines in their Assembly by John Rogers Herbert (1810-1890). If that doesn't show its stance, nothing will.

Well... Jewel was anti-Rome, true, but he was also far from Reformed; he was even more anti-Puritan than he was anti-Rome; he was vehemently anti-Geneva, absolutely committed to uniformity to the State Episcopal Church, under the Monarch as Supreme Governor. If he had lived until 1580, there is no doubt that he would have been anti-Separatist. If he had lived until 1633, 1644 or 1689, he would have been anti-Particular Baptist, and disagreed with both the First and Second Particular Baptist Confessions of Faith. His basis for doctrine and practice was Scripture as understood by the Fathers.

As a matter of history, by the end of Elizabeth's reign, most Puritans had thrown in the towel over reforming the Church, conformed,[8] and concentrated on preaching the law to try to turn Church conformists into regenerate men and women who lived by the Spirit. A task, though much praised by some today, was doomed to failure.[9] These conforming Puritans left it to the Separatists – men and women who are often unknown, ignored or despised today – to carry on the struggle.[10]

Was Jewel a Reformer? It would be closer to the mark to describe him as a staunch supporter, a pillar, a buttress, of the Established, corrupt (Protestant-Roman-Pagan) State Church – one hardly fitted to be a role model for a Calvinistic, Separatist Church today, one would think.

---

[8] William Perkins was in the van. William Haller: 'By careful avoidance of controverted questions in his public discourses, [he was able] to keep his pulpit until his death at forty-four in 1602' (William Haller: *The Rise of Puritanism... 1570-1643*, New York, 1947, p64, quoted by Patrick McGrath: *Papists and Puritans Under Elizabeth I*, Blandford Press, London, 1967, p327).

[9] M.M.Knappen: 'Though the moderates writhed and protested, though they continued to grasp at legal straws and fill books with theological arguments, they bowed their necks to the yoke'. (M.M.Knappen: *Tudor Puritanism*, Chicago 1939, reprinted 1963, p329, quoted by McGrath p363). 'They tried as best they could to swallow the Prayer Book, the Thirty-Nine Articles, and the Canons of 1604. Such were "the reluctant Puritans who were swept back into official fold of the disciplinary measures of 1605-6" and who "constituted a powerful Low Church wing of the Establishment... Through such agencies Puritan theological ideas, piety and moral attitudes could [,it was hoped, – DG] be communicated to the masses"' (McGrath p363, quoting Knappen p336. The fact is, 'the spread of popery and its influence at Court [under James 1] often gave the impression to Puritans and committed Protestants that it was they and not the Papists who were being encircled' (McGrath p373).

[10] See my *Battle*.

But because of his anti-Roman stance, all else is quietly forgotten, suppressed, ignored by Emmanuel. This is what I mean by 'The Case of the Curious Blind Spot'.

# Preacher: Postman or Pleader?

A preacher, opening his discourse on a passage of Scripture which was full of the gospel invitation and command, asked the congregation to look upon him as a postman[1] that day[2]. In saying this, he got his sermon underway on entirely the wrong foot.

Why? How?

A postman has to deliver the mail, faithfully and completely untampered with. That's his task. That's his only task. He has no interest in what he is delivering, whether or not the mail is wanted or hated, whether or not the recipient will do anything about it. The postman has done his job when he has pushed the mail through the letter box. He has no business to knock at the door, argue with the householder, plead with him to open the letter, read it and respond to it. Not at all! His job is to deliver the mail safe and sound, untampered with. That is all.

Whatever else a preacher is, however, most definitely he is not a postman. He is meant to do far more than merely deliver the text – in this case, the gospel invitation and command. He has to be faithful in his presentation of the gospel (1 Cor. 4:2; 2 Tim. 2:15), in his delivery, yes, of course, but – above all – he is meant to connect with his hearers, to touch their hearts, move them, persuade them, challenge, warn, encourage, exhort and seek to persuade them to obey the gospel – and, if they are unbelievers, to come to Christ. He must be the exact opposite of disinterested.[3] He must follow God in Christ and the apostles,[4] and show his love and concern for his hearers, his longing for

---

[1] US 'mailman'.
[2] I have produced this very brief – but I think important – article by slightly expanding material from my *The Secret Stifler*.
[3] Acts 18:4,13; 19:8,26; 20:21; 26:28-29; 28:23; Rom. 9:1-4; 10:1; 2 Cor. 5:11.
[4] Rom. 10:21; 2 Cor. 5:11,14,18-21; 6:1-2.

their spiritual welfare, his earnest desire for their benefit – even their salvation. And he must be pressing – wanting their conversion, under this sermon, now. And it must show.

Alas, today, we have far too many postman and far too few pleaders in the pulpit. Yes, we need the text laid out properly. Yes, we need the proper deductions to be made from the text. No question of it. But when that is done, the mail has been delivered, and that is all. Unless the preacher presses the gospel upon his hearers, he has failed. He has been a postman, nothing more; he has not been a pleader.

Take the Welsh Methodist preacher, Howell Harris (1714-1773). While not defending everything that he said, on the point I raise here, across the centuries Harris speaks today. Indeed, he cries out! He described the way he preached. He would open his discourse by explaining the text in its context, but in doing that he knew he was not preaching; he was waiting for 'the gale', 'the authority', to come upon him. By this, he meant the Spirit of God in power. But when the Spirit did come upon him, then, he would preach. But only then. Having explained the text, then, by the Spirit's enabling power, Harris would preach, really preach with 'authority', as he put it.

As I say, without endorsing every turn of phrase, Harris was right. We, today, need to catch some of his fire.

Reading sermons is utterly destructive of the vital distinction I am trying to make, and which Harris so graphically illustrated. Reading may be fine for accuracy, explanation, passing on of information – though I doubt it! – but to preach, to feel, and – above all – to make the hearers feel, to be persuaded, is a very, very different thing. Fiddling with a sheaf of notes, rustling sheets of paper, presenting a smooth and polished PowerPoint, delivering a boring, read-sermon drone, constitutes a very, very serious hindrance to preaching.

Preachers awake! We are not mere postmen. We MUST be pleaders! As was said of Robert Murray M'Cheyne, so it must be said of us: the hearers 'felt he was a'dying to have them converted'.

But let me close with Paul. Writing to the Thessalonian believers, the apostle set out what he was aiming for in his preaching, and how he measured success:

> Our gospel came to you not only in word, but also in power and in the Holy Spirit and with full conviction... You turned to God from idols to serve the living and true God, and to wait for his Son from heaven, whom he raised from the dead, Jesus who delivers us from the wrath to come (1 Thess. 1:5-10).

Nothing less will do.

# Touching the Untouchable:

# Observations on Evangelical Response to the Queen's Death

If I had been writing this 500 years ago in England, before the ink was dry I would have found myself incarcerated in the Tower; next stop, the gallows, or worse. There's little fear of that today, I'm relieved to say, but even so, because of what I write here, I suspect that I'll find a certain measure of hostility coming my way. After all, I am having the effrontery to touch the untouchable, to question the unquestionable.

As I write, Queen Elizabeth II has very recently died and been buried, and, quite naturally, the media has gone into overdrive. But so has the religious world, including evangelicals. It is the reaction of the latter which calls for a response. At least, that is my conviction.

I am not, in this article, concerned with the reactions of the leaders of the State Church to the Queen's passing, their comments, or their performance of political and religious acts in connection with it. The Established Church of England is an institution unequivocally founded on the Judaistic teaching of the Fathers.[1] So what else could be expected of the leaders of such? Think of it: Elizabeth Alexandra Mary Windsor, daughter of the Duke and Duchess of York, was born on 21st April 1926, born as every other procreated child is born; that is, as a sinner. She was christened – that is, religiously sprinkled with water – on 29th April 1926 by the then Archbishop of York, Cosmo Gordon Lang, in the Royal Chapel in Buckingham Palace. In accordance with the teaching of the Thirty-Nine Articles and The Book of Common Prayer of The Church of England, the baby Elizabeth, so it was claimed, was radically and

---

[1] See my *The Pastor*; *Battle*; *Priesthood*.

fundamentally transformed by this ritual: she was regenerated, taken out of Adam and brought into Christ. *First,* prayer was made to God for her:

> Give thy Holy Spirit to this infant, that she may be born again, and be made an heir of everlasting salvation, through our Lord Jesus Christ, who liveth and reigneth with thee and the Holy Spirit, now and for ever.

And after the administration of the rite, the priest categorically assured everybody of the effectiveness of this stupendous act:

> Seeing now, dearly beloved brethren, that this child is regenerate and grafted into the body of Christ's Church, let us give thanks unto Almighty God for these benefits, and with one accord make our prayers [for?] her, that this child may lead the rest of her life according to this beginning.[2]

Then, on 2nd June 1953, she was taken to the so-called house of God (Westminster Abbey) and placed into the hands of the highest officials of both State and Church. During the religious ceremony which followed, as the choir sang George Frideric Handel's anthem: 'Zadok the Priest and Nathan the Prophet Anointed Solomon King', the then Archbishop of Canterbury (Geoffrey Fisher) anointed her, transforming her from a mortal into a virtual god, and untouchable.[3] In short, by the priestly administration of the rites of the Established Church, Elizabeth Alexandra Mary Windsor had been regenerated as a baby, and, in early womanhood, made Supreme Governor of the Church of England, and Defender of the Faith.[4]

With such a pedigree – baptismally regenerated as an infant, and thus made a member of the Established Church, and later consecrated by anointing at the hand of the highest priest of the

---

[2] As with many others, the process was repeated for her great grandsons, George and Archie See my 'The BBC Gets It Wrong Again!' in my *New-Covenant Articles Volume Thirteen* and on my sermonaudio page.

[3] 'Touch not the LORD's anointed' (see 1 Chron. 16:22; Ps. 105:15).

[4] As was Charles II, James II, George IV, William IV and Edward VII, to name but a few.

Established Church to be made Supreme Governor of that Church – she must have been a child of God, mustn't she? What else?

Consequently, when she died and was buried, the response of the leaders of the State Church could only have been what it was. What else could it have been? The priests of the State Church, according to its doctrine, canons, rubrics and tradition, had taken this child out of Adam and taken her into Christ, and then transformed her into their Supreme Governor in matters spiritual. Imagine how shocking it would have been if, at her death, any officer of State or the Established Church had in any way expressed the merest whisper of a doubt about her spiritual condition and standing before God!

In all this, we have seen played out before our very eyes, the majestic, ceremonial flowering of a Christendom Church acting consistently with the Judaising doctrine of the Fathers upon whose teaching that institution is based.

Scripturally speaking, the mingling of the old and new covenants by the Fathers was a disaster of the first water.[5] Nevertheless, my point at this time is not to deal with this. Indeed, in recent days the Church of England and the State have acted consistently – in this respect, at least. And so I say no more about it at this time.

Nor am I interested in criticising the Queen. That is not why I write now. Inevitably, of course, she gets caught in the crossfire of what say. I am not trying to hide my view. But I am not setting myself up as her judge; Christ, and Christ alone, is that.

What does concern me in this article is the reaction of evangelicals to these solemn events, much of which has been exceedingly disturbing – to me, at least. Frankly, I have come across what I can only describe as overblown evangelical sentimentality, wishful thinking and straw clinging. Worse, I have met evangelical comment which displays unscriptural

---

[5] See my *The Pastor*; *Battle*.

thinking of a most serious and dangerous kind. It is this that I want to address. It is this that I am convinced must be addressed. I know I am touching the untouchable; questioning the unquestionable. I know I invite censure. But we dare not allow any confusion, vagueness or error over what constitutes a child of God. It matters not whether a sinner is born, lives and dies in a palace, or in a two up, two down; every human being is born a sinner in Adam and must be regenerated, must be brought in saving repentance to Christ, and must exercise a saving trust in Christ alone – in his person, work, sacrifice, his blood and righteousness – and so be a new creature in Christ. Or perish. The same goes for the Queen as for a tramp, for a prince as for a pauper, for a monarch as for a minion.

What is more – and this is the material point – infant sprinkling, the claim of baptismal regeneration,[6] a life of impeccable

---

[6] C.H.Spurgeon, in his famous (infamous, notorious, many at the time angrily thought it was) sermon on Mark 16:15-16, against baptismal regeneration, declared: 'Wherever the apostles went they met with obstacles to the preaching of the gospel, and the more open and effectual was the door of utterance the more numerous were the adversaries. These brave men who wielded the sword of the Spirit as to put to flight all their foes; and this they did not by craft and guile, but by making a direct cut at the error which impeded them. Never did they dream for a moment of adapting the gospel to the unhallowed tastes or prejudices of the people, but at once directly and boldly they brought down with both their hands the mighty sword of the Spirit upon the crown of the opposing error. This morning, in the name of the Lord of Hosts, my Helper and Defence, I shall attempt to do the same; and if I should provoke some hostility – if I should through speaking what I believe to be the truth lose the friendship of some and stir up the enmity of more, I cannot help it. The burden of the Lord is upon me, and I must deliver my soul. I have been loath enough to undertake the work, but I am forced to it by an awful and overwhelming sense of solemn duty. As I am soon to appear before my Master's bar, I will this day, if ever in my life, bear my testimony for truth, and run all risks. I am content to be cast out as evil if it must be so, but I cannot, I dare not, hold my peace. The Lord knows I have nothing in my heart but the purest love to the souls of those whom I feel imperatively called to rebuke sternly in the Lord's name. Among my hearers and readers, a

decency, religious talk and observance, Church attendance, keeping of vows, peerless honour, unquestioned sincerity and faultless dignity is not saving. It does not get even close to the biblical way of conversion and salvation.

Yet evangelicals have flown to their laptops to declare their confidence in the Queen's undoubted conversion to Christ, and justification by grace. In a culture where scriptural distinctives count for less and less among evangelicals, those evangelicals who have gone into print may not have used the actual words, but their intended meaning is clear: the Queen was indeed a child of God.

What evidence have evangelicals produced to justify their confident claims about the Queen's acceptable spiritual standing before God? None, to my mind, none that stands up, even though, it seems to me, many have scraped the barrel to find the best quotes they could. Despite all their efforts, nothing I have read fits the bill and demonstrates that the Queen was truly regenerate, truly trusting Christ's blood and righteousness alone for her salvation. If any reader can supply evidence to the opposite, I will, without delay, express my gratitude in print, acknowledge my mistake, and withdraw this article.

So much for the negative. Now for the positive. There is something far more serious in all this – and this is the major point that I want to make: by their quotations from the Queen's

---

considerable number will censure if not condemn me, but I cannot help it. If I forfeit your love for truth's sake I am grieved for you, but I cannot, I dare not, do otherwise. It is as much as my soul is worth to hold my peace any longer, and whether you approve or not I must speak out. Did I ever court your approbation? It is sweet to everyone to be applauded; but if for the sake of the comforts of respectability and the smiles of men any Christian minister shall keep back a part of his testimony, his Master at the last shall require it at his hands. This day, standing in the immediate presence of God, I shall speak honestly what I feel, as the Holy Spirit shall enable me; and I shall leave the matter with you to judge concerning it, as you will answer for that judgment at the last great day' (C.H.Spurgeon sermon 573). See my *Infant*; *The Hinge*; *Luther on Baptism*.

writings and speeches, and by their deductions – both implied and explicit – these evangelicals have given the clear impression that salvation from sin is obtained by a life of decency, by some kind of 'faith in God', by Church attendance, and by observance of rites, and performance of good works based on the ethics of Jesus. It is not! Let me remind you of the scriptural position. But before I do, let me very briefly make some important observations and define vital terms. My justifying arguments can be found in my works noted.

Justification means that a sinner is accounted, regarded as, made righteous in God's sight.[7]

This is by faith. Now there has been much talk of the Queen's 'faith in God' and 'her faith'. No vagueness can be tolerated at this point. Saving faith means 'trust' – trust in, reliance upon, Christ alone, his blood to wash from sin, his perfection to clothe and so present faultless in God's eyes.[8] The sinner's works or observances make no contribution to this justification – whether it be attempted obedience to God's law, or the keeping of *any* rules or standards; both essentially amount to the attempt to earn salvation by personal merit. And that is entirely unscriptural and utterly impossible for fallen men and women.

Now for the scriptures to establish all these points, and more:

> There is no distinction: for all have sinned and fall short of the glory of God, and are justified by his grace as a gift, through the redemption that is in Christ Jesus, whom God put forward as a propitiation by his blood, to be received by faith. This was to show God's righteousness, because in his divine forbearance he had passed over former sins. It was to show his righteousness at the present time, so that he might be just and the justifier of the one who has faith in Jesus.
> Then what becomes of our boasting? It is excluded. By what kind of law? By a law of works? No, but by the law of faith. For we hold that one is justified by faith apart from works of the law... God... will justify the circumcised by faith and the uncircumcised through faith (Rom. 3:22-30).

---

[7] See my *Justification*.
[8] See my *The Secret Stifler*; *No Safety*.

To the one who does not work but believes in him who justifies the ungodly, his faith is counted as righteousness, just as David also speaks of the blessing of the one to whom God counts righteousness apart from works: 'Blessed are those whose lawless deeds are forgiven, and whose sins are covered; blessed is the man against whom the Lord will not count his sin' (Rom. 4:5-8).

Gentiles who did not pursue righteousness have attained it, that is, a righteousness that is by faith; but... Israel who pursued a law that would lead to righteousness did not succeed in reaching that law. Why? Because they did not pursue it by faith, but as if it were based on works... Being ignorant of the righteousness of God, and seeking to establish their own, they did not submit to God's righteousness... Christ is the end of the law for righteousness to everyone who believes (Rom. 9:30-32; 10:3-4).

We know that a person is not justified by works of the law but through faith in Jesus Christ, so we also have believed in Christ Jesus, in order to be justified by faith in Christ and not by works of the law, because by works of the law no one will be justified... I do not nullify the grace of God, for if righteousness were through the law, then Christ died for no purpose (Gal. 2:16,21).

All who rely on works of the law are under a curse; for it is written: 'Cursed be everyone who does not abide by all things written in the book of the law, and do them'. Now it is evident that no one is justified before God by the law, for: 'The righteous shall live by faith'. But the law is not of faith, rather: 'The one who does them shall live by them'. Christ redeemed us from the curse of the law by becoming a curse for us – for it is written: 'Cursed is everyone who is hanged on a tree' – so that in Christ Jesus the blessing of Abraham might come to the Gentiles, so that we might receive the promised Spirit through faith (Gal. 3:10-14).

You were dead in the trespasses and sins in which you once walked, following the course of this world, following the prince of the power of the air, the spirit that is now at work in the sons of disobedience – among whom we all once lived in the passions of our flesh, carrying out the desires of the body and the mind, and were by nature children of wrath, like the rest of mankind. But God, being rich in mercy, because of the

great love with which he loved us, even when we were dead in
our trespasses, made us alive together with Christ – by grace
you have been saved – and raised us up with him and seated us
with him in the heavenly places in Christ Jesus, so that in the
coming ages he might show the immeasurable riches of his
grace in kindness toward us in Christ Jesus. For by grace you
have been saved through faith. And this is not your own doing;
it is the gift of God, not a result of works, so that no one may
boast (Eph. 2:1-9).

I am not saying the Queen boasted of her works for salvation.
Nor am I accusing her of relying on her works for salvation. I
cannot read any man's (or the Queen's) heart. But I am saying
that many evangelicals have spoken about her in such inflated
terms that they have given the inevitable impression that the
Queen was saved by her works, and, consequently, that
salvation *is* by works. And I deplore it. It is but the latest straw
piled on the growing heap of evidence showing that the biblical
doctrine of regeneration and conversion is being robbed of its
biblical distinction.[9]

* * *

I close with a few extracts. *First*, I will give some words of the
Queen as quoted in evangelical articles, words which the writers
chose to support their case (whether made explicitly or
implicitly) that the Queen did indeed savingly trust in Christ.
*Secondly*, I will quote from C.H.Spurgeon on the futility of any
sinner attempting salvation by works. *Thirdly*, I will leave the
last word to Christ himself. I make no comment on any of this. I
leave you, reader, to decide whether I have made the point.
Moreover, I hope this article may disabuse any who are in any
way trusting in their works to put them right with God. Saving
trust in Christ and his finished work is the only way. Above all,
what a joy it would be to know that, by reading this article,
some sinner had been awakened and turned to Christ, thereby
proving the truth of God's promise:

[9] See my *Conversion Ruined*; *Relationship Evangelism Exposed*; *A
Case of Mistaken Identity*.

Everyone who calls on the name of the Lord will be saved (Rom. 10:13).

And now for the extracts.

*The Queen's words as quoted by evangelicals*

*Christianity Today*:

> For me the teachings of Christ and my own personal accountability before God provide a framework in which I try to lead my life... I, like so many of you, have drawn great comfort in difficult times from Christ's words and example.
>
> I know just how much I rely on my own faith to guide me through the good times and the bad... Each day is a new beginning. I know that the only way to live my life is to try to do what is right, to take the long view, to give of my best in all that the day brings, and to put my trust in God.
>
> Faith plays a key role in the identity of millions of people, providing not only a system of belief but also a sense of belonging. It can act as a spur for social action. Indeed, religious groups have a proud track record of helping those in the greatest need, including the sick, the elderly, the lonely and the disadvantaged. They remind us of the responsibilities we have beyond ourselves.[10]
>
> Billions of people now follow Christ's teaching and find in him the guiding light for their lives. I am one of them because Christ's example helps me see the value in doing small things with great love, whoever does them and whatever they themselves believe.
>
> I have been – and remain – very grateful to... God for His steadfast love. I have indeed seen His faithfulness.[11]

---

[10] The Queen said this when 'celebrating her Diamond Jubilee in 2012, [and she] attended a multi-faith reception at Lambeth Palace, hosted by the Archbishop of Canterbury, featuring the leaders of eight faiths in the United Kingdom including Buddhism, Judaism, Islam and Hinduism'.

[11] Dudley Delfs: 'Died: Queen Elizabeth II, British Monarch Who Put Her Trust in God: In her seven-decade reign, she spoke regularly of the

*Christianity*:

> [Before her Coronation, she appealed to the nation:] Pray for
> me... that God may give me wisdom and strength to carry out
> the solemn promises I shall be making, and that I may
> faithfully serve Him and you, all the days of my life.

> I hope that, like me, you will be comforted by the example of
> Jesus of Nazareth who, often in circumstances of great
> adversity, managed to live an outgoing, unselfish and
> sacrificial life... He makes it clear that genuine human
> happiness and satisfaction lie more in giving than receiving;
> more in serving than in being served.

> This is the time of year when we remember that God sent his
> only Son[12] 'to serve, not to be served'. He restored love and
> service to the centre of our lives in the person of Jesus Christ. It
> is my prayer this Christmas Day that his example and teaching
> will continue to bring people together to give the best of
> themselves in the service of others. The carol, 'In the Bleak
> Midwinter', ends by asking a question of all of us who know
> the Christmas story, of how God gave himself to us in humble
> service: 'What can I give him, poor as I am?/If I were a
> shepherd, I would bring a lamb;/If I were a wise man, I would
> do my part...'. The carol gives the answer: 'Yet what I can I
> give him – give my heart'.[13]

I close this brief selection with an extract quoted in a tract by
Roger Carswell. Unlike the previous writers, Carswell made no
claim about the Queen's spiritual standing before God, but he
clearly selected the following words for a purpose:

> For many, this Christmas will not be easy. With our armed
> forces deployed around the world, thousands of service
> families face Christmas without their loved ones at home.

---

importance of her personal faith' (*Christianity Today*, 8th September
2022).

[12] Original 'son'.

[13] 'Queen Elizabeth's faith: Queen Elizabeth is known for her sense of
duty. She is head of the Church of England and has a genuine Christian
faith of her own' (*Christianity*).

The bereaved and the lonely will find it especially hard. And, as we all know, the world is going through difficult times. All this will affect our celebration of this great Christian festival.

Finding hope in adversity is one of the themes of Christmas. Jesus was born into a world full of fear. The angels came to frightened shepherds with hope in their voices: 'Fear not', they urged, 'we bring you tidings of great joy, which shall be to all people. For unto you is born this day in the city of David a Saviour who is Christ the Lord'.

Although we are capable of great acts of kindness, history teaches us that we sometimes need saving from ourselves – from our recklessness or our greed.

God sent into the world a unique person – neither a philosopher nor a general, important though they are, but a Saviour, with the power to forgive.

Forgiveness lies at the heart of the Christian faith. It can heal broken families, it can restore friendships and it can reconcile divided communities. It is in forgiveness that we feel the power of God's love.

In the last verse of this beautiful carol, 'O Little Town of Bethlehem', there's a prayer: 'O holy child of Bethlehem,/Descend to us we pray./Cast out our sin/and enter in./Be born in us today'.

It is my prayer that on this Christmas Day we might all find room in our lives for the message of the angels and for the love of God through Christ our Lord.[14]

## C.H.Spurgeon extract on Galatians 2:21:

The idea of salvation by the merit of our own works is exceedingly insinuating. It matters not how often it is refuted, it asserts itself again and again; and when it gains the least foothold it soon makes great advances. Hence Paul, who was determined to show it no quarter, opposed everything which bore its likeness. He was determined not to permit the thin end of the wedge to be introduced into the church, for well he knew that willing hands would soon be driving it home: hence when Peter sided with the Judaising party, and seemed to favour those who demanded that the Gentiles should be circumcised, our brave apostle withstood him to the face. He fought always

---

[14] Roger Carswell: 'Queen Elizabeth II: 1926 – 2022', DayOne and 10Publishing.

for salvation by grace through faith, and contended strenuously against all thought of righteousness by obedience to the law.[15] No-one could be more explicit than he upon the doctrine that we are not justified or saved by works in any degree, but solely by the grace of God. His trumpet gave forth no uncertain sound, but gave forth the clear note: 'By grace are you saved through faith; and that not of yourselves: it is the gift of God'. Grace meant grace with him, and he could not endure any tampering with the matter, or any frittering away of its meaning.

So fascinating is the doctrine of legal righteousness that the only way to deal with it is Paul's way. Stamp it out. Cry war to the knife against it. Never yield to it; but remember the apostle's firmness, and how stoutly he held his ground: 'To whom', says he, 'we gave place by subjection, no, not for an hour'.[16]

### Christ must have the last word

Two men went up into the temple to pray, one a Pharisee and the other a tax collector. The Pharisee, standing by himself, prayed thus: 'God, I thank you that I am not like other men, extortioners, unjust, adulterers, or even like this tax collector. I fast twice a week; I give tithes of all that I get'. But the tax collector, standing far off, would not even lift up his eyes to heaven, but beat his breast, saying: 'God, be merciful to me, a sinner!' I tell you, this man went down to his house justified, rather than the other. For everyone who exalts himself will be humbled, but the one who humbles himself will be exalted (Luke 18:10-14).

\* \* \*

As I said, I realise my words will offend. While I do not apologise, I wish to repeat what I said earlier.

I have not said the Queen boasted of her works for salvation. Nor have I accused her of relying on her works for salvation. I cannot read any man's (or the Queen's) heart. But I assert that

---

[15] Original 'obedience to the precepts of the ceremonial or the moral law'.

[16] C.H.Spurgeon sermon 1534.

many evangelicals have spoken about her in such inflated terms that they have given the inevitable impression that the Queen was saved by her works, and, consequently, that salvation *is* by works. And I deplore it.

# The Question Which Cannot Be Ducked

Christendom has ruined the new-covenant *ekklēsia*. I have made no bones about saying so. I have gone further: I have maintained that this past fifty years, evangelicals, by flirting with paganism, have seriously increased this Christendom adulteration of the *ekklēsia*.

The vast majority of believers, of course, never come across my work. And my guess is that most of the tiny minority which have read or heard something of mine on this subject have dismissed it – dismissed it, perhaps, as the mere babbling of some old curmudgeon, that geriatric, moaning, hard-of-hearing, dishevelled embarrassment sitting in the corner, the one who always spoils the family fun, who long ago ought to be have been put out to grass – treated kindly, perhaps, but not for a minute taken seriously.

Nevertheless, a few – and now we really are getting into the region of minuscule – have felt the force of what I have said, but the default position proves too strong for them. Very much like the converted Jews the writer of Hebrews addressed in his letter – those who felt the reclaiming magnetism power of the old covenant – I realise that the default, Christendom grip on most believers is almost unassailable. I feel it myself. Can we be free of it?

How safe Christendom appears! What a lovely face it wears – as long as you overlook its appalling record of hatred against the gospel and those who are determined to live by it and proclaim it. Dissent not allowed! And I am not putting Roman Christendom alone in the dock. Look how Reformed Christendom linked arms with the Roman to destroy the Anabaptists!

Even so, Christendom has the history, the tradition, all the big names, all the major Confessions, and all the rest of it, on its side. After nearly eighteen hundred years – how Christendom has stood the test of time! – it has flourished, proving that it is here to stay. Many simply like it that way, much as Judah liked their alternative to the Mosaic covenant (Jer. 5:30-31). Christendom is, like a pair of old slippers, just too comfortable.

I know my own heart! The scriptural path is risky; it demands thought; it asks too many questions. The traditional is all mapped out, cut and dried, all the questions answered, answered by experts, no less. Rome would not allow the *hoi polloi* to read Scripture for themselves; just accept what Mother Church says. Protestant Christendom can hardly be said to encourage enquiry. Absorb what you are told. Ritualism rules OK! Stick with what you know! Stick to what you are told! So many people can't be wrong, can they?

For all that, however, I know that I am not alone in issuing my alarums about the loss of *ekklēsia* life. And some, in a tentative hope of a move towards the recovery of the original, want to obey the biblical call for believers to flee from the Christendom Babylon (2 Cor. 6:14 – 7:1; Rev. 18:4). But I also know that they are puzzled. They have a question. How can we throw off Christendom and recover the *ekklēsia*? It becomes personal. What can I – me, personally – what can I do about promoting this recovery?

I am not inventing this dilemma. It is real; altogether, too real, I am afraid. Such questions have been put to me. Indeed, I have them myself.

I think the short answer must be that there is nothing that we can do to throw off Christendom and get back to the *ekklēsia*; at least, not on any scale. Frankly, I cannot conceive that the Christendom juggernaut is even aware of anything that I can throw at it, let alone be disturbed by any word of mine. The recovery of the *ekklēsia*, the believer's liberation from the toils of Christendom, is beyond the power and wit of man. God's word through Zechariah to Zerubbabel applies: 'Not by might, nor by power, but by my Spirit, says the LORD of hosts' (Zech. 4:6; see also Hos. 1:7).

In any case, in a sense it is impossible for any individual to return to the *ekklēsia*; *ekklēsia* life needs the two or three (Matt. 18:15-20).

Please do not misunderstand me. Prayer is open to us, prayer, trusting in God's sovereignty. We need look no further than Daniel 9:1-19 for that. Moreover, since Christ loved and died for the *ekklēsia* (Eph. 5:25-32), who can care for the *ekklēsia* more than he?

But that answer, in my view, is still ducking the question.

I am sure that although the unravelling of Christendom and the recovery of the *ekklēsia* is beyond us, in whatever way we can, however feeble our efforts may be, we must go on keeping the issue before our fellow-believers. At times, the prophets must have felt they were flogging a dead horse[1] – Isaiah certainly did (Isa. 49:4; 53:1),[2] but they kept on. And on.

If I may speak personally, although I am no prophet, in my discourses and in my articles and books, I try to keep the issue in the public square. I ask you, reader: What can you do? Whatever it is, 'whatever your hand finds to do, do it with your might... In the morning sow your seed, and at evening withhold not your hand, for you do not know which will prosper, this or that, or whether both alike will be good' (Eccles. 9:10; 11:6). God is sovereign, but he usually works through instruments, weak instruments at that. Widows can cast their mites into the treasury; a lad can give his picnic lunch; a David with a pebble can defeat a Goliath. Let us go on, even against impossible odds. I draw comfort from – and find a challenge in – 1 Peter 1:10-12. The prophets knew they were prophesying about things they would not live to experience, but even so they laboured on, and were deeply curious and concerned about what God was showing them, even though he told them it was not for their day.

---

[1]   Useful idioms abound: wall writing, bursting bubbles, wind/whirlwind, and so on. See the later notes.

[2]   The fact that at least one of these verses is messianic only adds poignancy.

But even in this there is a dilemma. To help others to see what we have lost by Christendom, I need to approach Christendom, get involved with it, use it in some way or another. This is a paradox I labour with.

Yet, even in admitting that much, I am still evading the real problem, the real issue. It is not the Christendom out there; it's the Christendom in here – that is, in me. As I have hinted in passing, that's the hardest nut of the lot to crack. Me! Self! I know it's true that God works by contraries; I preach it and write about it. I know that in God's terms, small is great, weak is strong, humble is powerful, the despised flourishes (1 Cor. 1:18 – 2:16). I protest against preaching centres, the galaxy of star preachers, watching the ratings, the love of the big, packed auditorium, and all the rest of modern evangelical razzmatazz. But – and here's the real battle – these criticisms of Christendom my head may hold, and my tongue and my pen may proclaim, but Christendom, being ingrained within me, is too powerful for me to throw off; its pernicious and insidious influence is too strong for me. I preach and write about walking in the Spirit in the new covenant, but do I really want to be rid of Christendom's goodies? That's the real issue for me. It's not 'them'; it's me.

Despite all this, I have not lost hope; not quite. Why not?

Because, if I am right in saying that in the past fifty years evangelical opinion-formers, with their dependence on paganised-Christendom, have been in the van of corrupting the *ekklēsia* even more devastatingly than it was, then I draw an odd – even perverse – encouragement from the history of Israel. Israel did something similar in the days of the old covenant: they corrupted their covenant by consorting with pagans and paganism. Well, that in itself is no comfort! No. It is not. But it's what God did about it! God made sure that if Israel would not learn the lesson through the words of the prophets, then Israel would learn the lesson when paganism came back to bite Israel, and bite Israel hard – as it did. One example out of many must suffice. Israel disobeyed God and went to Egypt for help –

very much like modern evangelicals have gone to pagans to help them run the church to make it and its message acceptable to the carnal. God publicly addressed Egypt through the prophet – publicly so that Israel could hear it:

> You have been a staff of reed to the house of Israel, when they grasped you with the hand, you broke and tore all their shoulders; and when they leaned on you, you broke and made all their loins to shake (Ezek. 29:6-7).

Although Israel would not listen, God made sure that the chickens came home to roost.[3] It would take time, but Israel and Judah, because of their departure from the covenant, were on the road to captivity. I know that after seventy years Judah returned from Babylon, but it was never the same (Ez. 3:12; Zech. 4:10; Hag. 2:3). And what a wretched seventy years (Ps. 137)!

I am no prophet, as I have said, but it would not surprise me if we are heading for something similar. Indeed, even as I write, straws are blowing in the wind.[4] Paul told the Corinthians that Israel's sin and God's judgment were meant to warn them as believers, and make them reform (1 Cor. 10:1-22). If ever there was a day when believers needed to take this passage seriously, that day is now.

What I am saying is this: having been fawned on by the church, having proved so 'helpful' in the church's drive to make itself and the gospel attractive to pagans, State Christendom will demand its pound of flesh.[5] Take, for instance, tax relief. I speak of what I know in the UK, but I think something similar applies across the Atlantic. The Christendom State is willing to grant churches tax relief, among other benefits, yes, but it expects, it demands, a *quid pro quo*. If the State grants the churches money, or whatever, the churches must conform to the State's dictat over church governance, church discipline, gender issues, safeguarding, sexual behaviour, the content of sermons, guidance and rulings given to members; in all such matters,

---

[3] See earlier note.
[4] See the previous note.
[5] See the previous note.

churches will have to comply with whatever pagans demand. He who pays the piper...[6] As I write, these things are happening. The State is beginning to tell the churches what they can and what they can't do. What they must do.

The only hope? That if we believers will not wake up to our disobedience to Scripture, stop our headlong descent into disaster, then, maybe, the State, Christendom, will do it for us. How? By exacting too-high a price for what it is offering, demanding far more from the church than the benefit it offers – thus, at long last, stirring believers to dig their heels in, and pin their ears back, and say enough is enough! Whereupon, Christendom will turn quickly from being a Father Christmas to being a Nero; the present whimsy will be replaced by a terrifying, bleak grimness. And the result? Persecution! This, too, has happened, time and again.[7]

And herein lies my hope for the *ekklēsia*. Persecution! Persecution – not popularity – was always meant to be the norm for the *ekklēsia*.[8] The *ekklēsia* thrives under persecution.[9] Under

---

[6] See the previous note.

[7] The history of the persecuted down the centuries is there for all to read. History, of course, is written by the winners, but truth will out. For my small contribution, see my *Battle*.

[8] See 'The Fundamental Flaw' in my *Relationship Evangelism Exposed*; 'Separation in the New Covenant' in my *Public Worship: God-Ordained or Man-Invented?* See also my *Battle*.

[9] This teaching can be found throughout the New Testament. Take one example: 'Count it all joy, my brothers, when you meet trials of various kinds, for you know that the testing of your faith produces steadfastness. And let steadfastness have its full effect, that you may be perfect and complete, lacking in nothing... Blessed is the man who remains steadfast under trial, for when he has stood the test he will receive the crown of life, which God has promised to those who love him... Be patient, therefore, brothers, until the coming of the Lord.... As an example of suffering and patience, brothers, take the prophets who spoke in the name of the Lord. Behold, we consider those blessed who remained steadfast. You have heard of the steadfastness of Job, and you have seen the purpose of the Lord, how the Lord is compassionate and merciful' (Jas. 1:2-4,12; 5:7,10-11).

persecution, the church goes underground; it becomes secret, hidden, separate, despised and all the rest, believers really do become 'strangers' and 'aliens' in the world (Heb. 11:13; 1 Pet. 1:1,17; 2:11),[10] yes, but this means that the church really does become the *ekklēsia*![11] Christ made it plain:

> If you were of the world, the world would love you as its own; but because you are not of the world, but I chose you out of the world, therefore the world hates you (John 15:19).

And, shortly after saying this, in his great prayer he declared:

> I have manifested your name to the people whom you gave me out of the world... I am not praying for the world but for those whom you have given me, for they are yours... I have given them your word, and the world has hated them because they are not of the world, just as I am not of the world. I do not ask that you take them out of the world, but that you keep them from the evil one. They are not of the world, just as I am not of the world. Sanctify them in the truth; your word is truth. As you sent me into the world, so I have sent them into the world (John 17:6-18).

The trash of Christendom trimmings will drop away from the church when persecution is unleashed upon it, and the church will once again come closer to being what it should be – separate from the world.

I realise persecution will be painful, to put it mildly and to state the glaringly obvious, but this, I am convinced, is the only hope. Knowing my weakness, I dread it. But it may well be God's way. Consequently, while I understand their concern, I find myself somewhat out of step with believers who endlessly moan

---

[10] But not to God: 'You are no longer strangers and aliens, but you are fellow-citizens with the saints and members of the household of God, built on the foundation of the apostles and prophets, Christ Jesus himself being the cornerstone, in whom the whole structure, being joined together, grows into a holy temple in the Lord. In him you also are being built together into a dwelling place for God by the Spirit' (Eph. 2:19-22).
[11] See my *Public Worship: God-Ordained or Man-Invented?* and *Public Worship Notes.*

about persecution and pray for its removal. Even more resolutely do I disagree with their petitioning the State to lift it. It might well be that by persecution God is answering his people's prayer for a recovery of the new covenant. Think of that! While I reject the deliberate courting of persecution, we must stop the present madness – not to say, sinfulness – of soliciting popularity from the world, and coveting the world's help and applause. God doesn't need the world's praise or support! I am bold to say that if believers start to be different to the world, live separated from the world, and churches show a willingness to return to the new covenant, this will in itself lead to persecution, and this will, in turn, advance the further return to the new covenant: a truly virtuous circle.

That is my answer to the question: 'What can we do about throwing off Christendom?'

I realise that this, too, will probably be dismissed as mere hogwash. Or alarmist. But to warn of persecution is not to want it or invite it. There is no need for it. The *ekklēsia* at Corinth had seriously defected from the new covenant but, we may hope, for a time at least it responded to Paul's letters of rebuke, warning and calls for reform. Alas, as for the various *ekklēsias* of Revelation 2 & 3, they, I am afraid, had their candlesticks removed. The lesson from Israel and the *ekklēsias* of the New Testament is patent.

If any readers remain unconvinced, may I close by leaving them with a thought which may cause them to lose some sleep? What if – and in the UK this is not such a laughable suggestion as it would have been a few years back – what if Islam should get its hands on the levers of power in the State? What if the Sharia merchants should replace the present liberal, insipid Christendom hawkers? We in the UK have too long 'enjoyed' the 'protection' of a benign Christendom. What if that summer should give way to winter?

I do not publish this article to close the debate. Rather, I want to provoke it. Reader, what is your answer to the question? How can we believers get free of the Christendom church, and find something at least approximating to the *ekklēsia*? Can we? Will we?

# A Disaster Averted:
# Romans 14:5-6

I start by quoting the entire relevant passage in Romans, not just the selected verses in the title. It is vital to see the whole thing in context, the big picture:

> As for the one who is weak in faith, welcome him, but not to quarrel over opinions. One person believes he may eat anything, while the weak person eats only vegetables. Let not the one who eats despise the one who abstains, and let not the one who abstains pass judgment on the one who eats, for God has welcomed him. Who are you to pass judgment on the servant of another? It is before his own master that he stands or falls. And he will be upheld, for the Lord is able to make him stand.
>
> One person esteems one day as better than another, while another esteems all days alike. Each one should be fully convinced in his own mind. The one who observes the day, observes it in honour of the Lord. The one who eats, eats in honour of the Lord, since he gives thanks to God, while the one who abstains, abstains in honour of the Lord and gives thanks to God. For none of us lives to himself, and none of us dies to himself. For if we live, we live to the Lord, and if we die, we die to the Lord. So then, whether we live or whether we die, we are the Lord's. For to this end Christ died and lived again, that he might be Lord both of the dead and of the living.
>
> Why do you pass judgment on your brother? Or you, why do you despise your brother? For we will all stand before the judgment seat of God; for it is written: 'As I live, says the Lord, every knee shall bow to me, and every tongue shall confess to God'. So then each of us will give an account of himself to God.
>
> Therefore let us not pass judgment on one another any longer, but rather decide never to put a stumbling block or hindrance in the way of a brother. I know and am persuaded in the Lord Jesus that nothing is unclean in itself, but it is unclean for anyone who thinks it unclean. For if your brother is grieved by what you eat, you are no longer walking in love. By what you eat, do not destroy the one for whom Christ died. So do not let

what you regard as good be spoken of as evil. For the kingdom of God is not a matter of eating and drinking but of righteousness and peace and joy in the Holy Spirit. Whoever thus serves Christ is acceptable to God and approved by men. So then let us pursue what makes for peace and for mutual up-building.

Do not, for the sake of food, destroy the work of God. Everything is indeed clean, but it is wrong for anyone to make another stumble by what he eats. It is good not to eat meat or drink wine or do anything that causes your brother to stumble. The faith that you have, keep between yourself and God. Blessed is the one who has no reason to pass judgment on himself for what he approves. But whoever has doubts is condemned if he eats, because the eating is not from faith. For whatever does not proceed from faith is sin.

We who are strong have an obligation to bear with the failings of the weak, and not to please ourselves. Let each of us please his neighbour for his good, to build him up. For Christ did not please himself, but as it is written: 'The reproaches of those who reproached you fell on me'. For whatever was written in former days was written for our instruction, that through endurance and through the encouragement of the Scriptures we might have hope. May the God of endurance and encouragement grant you to live in such harmony with one another, in accord with Christ Jesus, that together you may with one voice glorify the God and Father of our Lord Jesus Christ. Therefore welcome one another as Christ has welcomed you, for the glory of God (Rom. 14:1 – 15:7).

I have become convinced that the problem in Rome, which Paul was dealing with in Romans 14 and 15 – and it was a thorny problem within the *ekklēsia* at Rome – arose because some converted Jews, even though they were living in the day of the new covenant, felt they ought to keep alive some of their familiar (and, no doubt, well-loved) Jewish customs, traditions, prohibitions, and the like, vestiges of the old, Mosaic covenant.[1] Other believers rightly saw no need for this, and might well

---

[1] Hebrews was written to prevent Jewish believers leaving Christ, leaving the new covenant, and returning to the old covenant. That, it surely does not need to be said, would have been a disaster of the first magnitude.

have thought strongly about it. How would the two groups get on? How could the *ekklēsia* survive? Would it? That was the issue at Rome. And that is why Paul wrote this section of his letter.

The problem, of course, was not confined to Rome; it was a widespread, major – and very sensitive – issue for the first believers in general – who were, of course, overwhelmingly converted Jews.[2] And when Gentiles were being converted, followed by the eruption of the teaching of the false brothers – the *pseudadelphoi* (2 Cor. 11:26; Gal. 2:4-5) – with their insistence that Gentiles must be committed to some basic observance of old-covenant principles and practices if they were to be saved (Acts 15:1; Gal. 2:1*ff.*), the issue was exasperated, and sensitive feelings were aroused to boiling point.[3] The *ekklēsia* in Galatia, in Corinth, in Colosse, *et al*, had problems over the ramifications of the new covenant. And the Jewish believers to whom the writer of Hebrews addressed his treatise were in serious trouble over the discontinuity between the two covenants. But when the *pseudadelphoi* got to work, a crisis of a tender conscience was rapidly escalated into a divisive problem of major dimensions, one, which held within it the potential for very serious and long-term damage to the gospel. The *pseudadelphoi* were acting irresponsibly – as children playing with matches in a powder mill.

Paul, moved by the Spirit, could see the far-reaching nature of the issues that were involved, and clearly saw the consequences which would follow if the *pseudadelphoi* won the day. And so

---

[2] Even before *pseudadelphoi* (see below) got to work, the Greek and Hebrew Jews who had been converted found living together posed real problems for them (Acts 6:1-7). One might comment: 'Naturally!' And in more than one sense. Think! If Jews from different cultures – but Jews nevertheless – found it hard, on conversion to Christ, to live in harmony with each other, avoid suspicion, and start firing accusations like grapeshot, what must it have meant for Jews and Gentiles to find themselves one in Christ? Jews and Gentiles! Think of the history of the Middle East! Think of the troubled history of the Jews, full stop!

[3] See my *False Brothers: Paul and Today*.

he dealt with it.[4] But, of course, the issue remained a hot potato for some time. To add another metaphor from the world of heat, the risk did not melt away like snow in June. And to pick up on a previous image, if the spark had touched a powder keg, the gospel – and the *ekklēsia* – would have been blown to smithereens.

In facing and countering the teaching of the *pseudadelphoi*, both Paul and the writer of Hebrews[5] were adamant that Christ had come to fulfil the old covenant; that is, he had fulfilled all the shadows of the old covenant and established them in reality, in substance – all of them – in a spiritual sense, thus establishing the new covenant. We are talking about tabernacle, temple, priesthood, sacrifice, sabbath, feasts, altar, prophets, possession of the land... all existed in the old covenant, all were temporarily instituted by God for Israel for the duration of the old covenant,[6] and in order to give the Jews pictures, illustrations, foreshadows and types of Christ. But in the new covenant, Christ – the person and work of Christ himself – is the living embodiment of them all; and he, bringing all the shadows to their God-intended end, has brought in their eternal, spiritual reality, in their substantial, permanent fulfilment. They were the shadow; he is the substance (Matt. 5:17; Col. 2:17; Heb. 7:11-12,18-22; 8:5,13; 9:15; 10:1,9; 12:18-24). It can be summed up in one word, one person: Christ. As Paul declared: 'Christ is all' (Col. 3:11). The upshot: Christ rendered the old covenant obsolete (Heb. 8:13). He is the new covenant (Isa. 42:6; 49:8); he is all.

But, as we all know only too well, it's the living out of any doctrine that is the real issue.[7] In saying that, I am speaking

---

[4] I have written and spoken on this and associated issues a number of times. See, especially, my *False*; *Christ Is All*. Also, many items on my sermonaudio.com page.

[5] Not that the writer of Hebrews ever refers to them, but had their teaching percolated to his readers, and encouraged them in their defection?

[6] On the temporary nature of the old covenant, see my *Three Verses*.

[7] William Cowper, writing on 'That God is love, and changes not,/Nor knows the shadow of a turn', commented: 'Sweet truth, and easy to

about us, today. Doctrine may be discussed in ivory towers, delivered in polished sermons over pulpit desks, but it's down on the ground, among the occupiers of the pews (and, of course, as well as those aforesaid towers and pulpits) where it has to be worked out in daily action.

\* \* \*

Let me summarise what the New Testament tells us of the life of the early *ekklēsia* in regard to this Jewish/Gentile question. And it was a Jewish/Gentile question: that was the fundamental issue. All sorts of ingredients went into the mix, of course, but, at bottom, it was a racial problem, with the overriding factor of the transition between the old and new covenants; in itself, that was a radical discontinuity which required many passages of apostolic instruction to fix firmly in the thought and practice of believers. Both Jews and Gentiles were, in an instant – by regeneration, conversion, union with Christ – taken out their old comfort-zones (very different, they were, too) and transferred into a totally different environment, something that until then would have been utterly unthinkable – reprehensible, indeed – to both parties. No wonder some of them felt apprehensive. It's simply down to God's grace, and entirely by the effective working of his Spirit, that under such explosive circumstances the *ekklēsia* survived – let alone thrived.

Concerning the radical newness of the new covenant, Paul was adamant. Christ, in the new covenant, has abolished all distinctions between Jew and Gentile. What a contrast to the old covenant – which God designed (yes, designed) to distinguish and separate Jew and Gentile, and repeatedly insisted that Israel maintain that separation.[8] In that covenant (and before), a

---

repeat!/But when my faith is sharply tried/I find myself a learner yet,/Unskilful, weak, and apt to slide'.

[8] God sent prophet after prophet to warn and exhort Israel to stay separate from pagans. See my *Evangelicals Warned*. As countless passages of the Old Testament make plain, it was because both Israel and Judah failed to keep separate from the pagans, but adulterated the

Gentile had to become a virtual Jew to benefit (Gen. 17:11-13; Ex. 12:43-49; Num. 9:14; 15:15-16).[9]

In Christ, all is changed. As Paul put it, in the new age, the age of the Spirit, all the old Jewish distinctives – not excluding, the especially thorny ones of circumcision, sabbath, kosher food, festivals, dates – have disappeared. To return to such things is puerile, and to make an issue of such things is dangerous and – and here's the punch word – sinful:

> Therefore let us not pass judgment on one another any longer, but rather decide never to put a stumbling block or hindrance in the way of a brother. I know and am persuaded in the Lord Jesus that nothing is unclean in itself, but it is unclean for anyone who thinks it unclean. For if your brother is grieved by what you eat, you are no longer walking in love. By what you eat, do not destroy the one for whom Christ died. So do not let what you regard as good be spoken of as evil. For the kingdom of God is not a matter of eating and drinking but of righteousness and peace and joy in the Holy Spirit. Whoever thus serves Christ is acceptable to God and approved by men. So then let us pursue what makes for peace and for mutual up-building.
> Do not, for the sake of food, destroy the work of God. Everything is indeed clean, but it is wrong for anyone to make another stumble by what he eats. It is good not to eat meat or drink wine or do anything that causes your brother to stumble. The faith that you have, keep between yourself and God. Blessed is the one who has no reason to pass judgment on himself for what he approves. But whoever has doubts is condemned if he eats, because the eating is not from faith. For whatever does not proceed from faith is sin.
> We who are strong have an obligation to bear with the failings of the weak, and not to please ourselves. Let each of us please his neighbour for his good, to build him up. For Christ did not please himself, but as it is written: 'The reproaches of those who reproached you fell on me'. For whatever was written in former days was written for our instruction, that through

---

covenant by fraternising with pagans and their paganism, that both were taken into captivity.

[9] The book of Ruth shows the practical outworking of such a transformation.

endurance and through the encouragement of the Scriptures we might have hope. May the God of endurance and encouragement grant you to live in such harmony with one another, in accord with Christ Jesus, that together you may with one voice glorify the God and Father of our Lord Jesus Christ. Therefore welcome one another as Christ has welcomed you, for the glory of God (Rom. 14:13-23; 15:1-5).

Do not forget the heavy personal price Paul had to pay over Peter's failure to keep to new-covenant principles when he publicly rebuked Peter, and the courage he showed in doing it:

When Cephas [that is, Peter] came to Antioch, I opposed him to his face, because he stood condemned. For before certain men came from James, he was eating with the Gentiles; but when they came he drew back and separated himself, fearing the circumcision party. And the rest of the Jews acted hypocritically along with him, so that even Barnabas was led astray by their hypocrisy. But when I saw that their conduct was not in step with the truth of the gospel, I said to Cephas before them all: 'If you, though a Jew, live like a Gentile and not like a Jew, how can you force the Gentiles to live like Jews?' (Gal. 2:11-14).

In his writings, too, Paul repeatedly spelled out the position. Believers – whether they had been Jews or Gentiles before conversion – are new men in Christ (2 Cor. 5:17), citizens of heaven (Phil. 3:20), one in Christ, and the practical effect of this must be maintained and fostered at all times:

Just as the body is one and has many members, and all the members of the body, though many, are one body, so it is with Christ. For in one Spirit we were all baptised into one body – Jews or Greeks, slaves or free – and all were made to drink of one Spirit (1 Cor. 12:12-13).

It is those of faith who are the sons of Abraham [Paul clearly had in mind God's promise to Abraham (Gen. 12:3): 'In you all the families of the earth shall be blessed']... Christ redeemed us... so that in Christ Jesus the blessing of Abraham might come to the Gentiles, so that we might receive the promised Spirit through faith... There is neither Jew nor Greek, there is neither slave nor free, there is no male and female, for you are all one in Christ Jesus. And if you are Christ's, then you are Abraham's offspring, heirs according to promise...

In Christ Jesus neither circumcision nor uncircumcision counts for anything, but only faith working through love...

Neither circumcision counts for anything, nor uncircumcision, but a new creation (Gal. 3:7,13-14,28-29; 5:6; 6:15).[10]

[God] has delivered us from the domain of darkness and transferred us to the kingdom of his beloved Son...

In him the whole fullness of deity dwells bodily, and you have been filled in him, who is the head of all rule and authority. In him also you were circumcised with a circumcision made without hands, by putting off the body of the flesh, by the circumcision of Christ, having been buried with him in [spiritual] baptism,[11] in which you were also raised with him through faith in the powerful working of God, who raised him from the dead. And you, who were dead in your trespasses and the uncircumcision of your flesh, God made alive together with him, having forgiven us all our trespasses, by cancelling the record of debt [the law] that stood against us with its legal demands. This he set aside, nailing it to the cross. He disarmed the rulers and authorities and put them to open shame, by triumphing over them in him.

Therefore let no one pass judgment on you in questions of food and drink, or with regard to a festival or a new moon or a sabbath. These are a shadow of the things to come, but the substance belongs to Christ. Let no one disqualify you, insisting on asceticism and worship of angels, going on in detail about visions, puffed up without reason by his sensuous mind, and not holding fast to the Head, from whom the whole body, nourished and knit together through its joints and ligaments, grows with a growth that is from God...

Here there is not Greek and Jew, circumcised and uncircumcised, barbarian, Scythian, slave, free; but Christ is all, and in all (Col. 1:13; 2:9-19; 3:11).

Perhaps the apostle's fullest statement on the practical side of this momentous change may be found in these words:

---

[10] Do not miss the point: in the new covenant, 'neither circumcision nor uncircumcision counts for anything'; neither Jewishness nor un-Jewishness matters a bean. Nor do any of the other divisions mentioned in the text.

[11] See my *Infant: Baptist Sacramentalism*.

Remember that at one time you Gentiles in the flesh, called 'the uncircumcision' by what is called the circumcision, which is made in the flesh by hands – remember that you were at that time separated from Christ, alienated from the commonwealth of Israel and strangers to the covenants of promise, having no hope and without God in the world. But now in Christ Jesus you who once were far off have been brought near by the blood of Christ. For he himself is our peace, who has made us both one and has broken down in his flesh the dividing wall of hostility by abolishing the law of commandments expressed in ordinances, that he might create in himself one new man in place of the two, so making peace, and might reconcile us both to God in one body through the cross, thereby killing the hostility. And he came and preached peace to you who were far off and peace to those who were near. For through him we both have access in one Spirit to the Father. So then you are no longer strangers and aliens, but you are fellow citizens with the saints and members of the household of God, built on the foundation of the apostles and prophets, Christ Jesus himself being the cornerstone, in whom the whole structure, being joined together, grows into a holy temple in the Lord. In him you also are being built together into a dwelling place for God by the Spirit (Eph. 2:11-22).

In his great mediatorial prayer, Christ specifically asked for all believers 'that they may all be one' (John 17:21). In due time, in accordance with Christ's promise (John 14:16-26; 15:26-27; 16:7-15), Paul fully fleshed out the change in covenant which brought this about – Jewish (old-covenant) observances (including the sabbath), slavery, dietary laws... all are abolished, fulfilled, made redundant in Christ. Converted Jews and Gentiles, being one in Christ, no longer have any barrier wall between them.

And the writer of the letter to the Hebrews left no wriggle room for doubt:

On the one hand, a former commandment is set aside because of its weakness and uselessness (for the law made nothing perfect); but on the other hand, a better hope is introduced, through which we draw near to God.
And it was not without an oath. For those who formerly became priests were made such without an oath, but this one

was made a priest with an oath by the one who said to him: 'The LORD has sworn and will not change his mind, "You are a priest forever"'. This makes Jesus the guarantor of a better covenant.

The former priests were many in number, because they were prevented by death from continuing in office, but he holds his priesthood permanently, because he continues forever. Consequently, he is able to save to the uttermost those who draw near to God through him, since he always lives to make intercession for them.

For it was indeed fitting that we should have such a high priest, holy, innocent, unstained, separated from sinners, and exalted above the heavens. He has no need, like those high priests, to offer sacrifices daily, first for his own sins and then for those of the people, since he did this once for all when he offered up himself. For the law appoints men in their weakness as high priests, but the word of the oath, which came later than the law, appoints a Son who has been made perfect forever (Heb. 7:18-28).

Christ has obtained a ministry that is as much more excellent than the old as the covenant he mediates is better, since it is enacted on better promises. For if that first covenant had been faultless, there would have been no occasion to look for a second.

For he finds fault with them when he says: 'Behold, the days are coming, declares the Lord, when I will establish a new covenant with the house of Israel and with the house of Judah, not like the covenant that I made with their fathers on the day when I took them by the hand to bring them out of the land of Egypt. For they did not continue in my covenant, and so I showed no concern for them, declares the Lord. For this is the covenant that I will make with the house of Israel after those days, declares the Lord: I will put my laws into their minds, and write them on their hearts, and I will be their God, and they shall be my people. And they shall not teach, each one his neighbour and each one his brother, saying, 'Know the Lord,' for they shall all know me, from the least of them to the greatest. For I will be merciful toward their iniquities, and I will remember their sins no more'.

In speaking of a new covenant, he makes the first one obsolete. And what is becoming obsolete and growing old is ready to vanish away (Heb. 8:6-13).

> The law has but a shadow of the good things to come instead of
> the true form of these realities... [Christ] does away with the
> first in order to establish the second... (Heb. 10:1-18).

Christ fulfilled the old covenant and rendered it obsolete,
establishing the new. Believers, therefore, are not under the law,
not under the old covenant; they are new men under the new
covenant:

> Sin will have no dominion over you, since you are not under
> law but under grace. What then? Are we to sin because we are
> not under law but under grace? By no means!... (Rom. 6:14-
> 23).

> ...My brothers, you also have died to the law through the body
> of Christ, so that you may belong to another, to him who has
> been raised from the dead, in order that we may bear fruit for
> God. For while we were living in the flesh, our sinful passions,
> aroused by the law, were at work in our members to bear fruit
> for death. But now we are released from the law, having died to
> that which held us captive, so that we serve in the new way of
> the Spirit and not in the old way of the written code (Rom. 7:1-
> 6).

Such is the massive discontinuity between the two covenants,
old and new. It goes without saying that the staggering nature of
that change must have been most keenly felt in the early days of
the new age, and most sharply experienced by the early converts
from among the Jews and Gentiles. We contemporary believers
have, for good or ill, well-nigh two millennia of tradition to look
back on, many examples – good and bad – to learn from; the
first believers were plunged into the deep end, and it was they
who had to learn to tread water in the drastically new
environment. No wonder the new covenant ought to be thought
of as the age of the Spirit. Only he could bring such a change
into practical effect.

It surely goes without saying that those believers, on their
conversion, were not suddenly turned into men and women who
were absolutely and utterly delivered from all their previous
prejudices and biases. And my use of 'were' can be – must be –
replaced by 'are'. Believers *are* a new creation, and all things

have become new (2 Cor. 5:17) for believers today – or should be so in practical effect. Yes, but it takes a life-time of continual progressive sanctification for believers to be increasingly transformed into Christ-likeness in daily life. But that conformity to Christ was always God's purpose (Rom. 8:28-30).[12] Believers soon discover that they are on a learning-curve, having to leave their familiar and much-loved cultural-baggage standing on the platform, while the gospel train they have just boarded picks up speed, powering its way towards the anticipated terminus. And this certainly applied in the early days when the Jewish/Gentile question was raging. No wonder then that Paul felt the need to urge believers:

> I therefore, a prisoner for the Lord, urge you to walk in a manner worthy of the calling to which you have been called, with all humility and gentleness, with patience, bearing with one another in love, eager to maintain the unity of the Spirit in the bond of peace. There is one body and one Spirit – just as you were called to the one hope that belongs to your call – one Lord, one faith, one baptism, one God and Father of all, who is over all and through all and in all (Eph. 4:1-6).

* * *

Clearly, although Christ ended one covenant and established another,[13] the inauguration of this once-for-all (Heb. 10:10) change produced an inevitable time of transition and adjustment. Let me illustrate. Although we are taught history as a matter of dates, the actual living-out of history, in reality, in practice, at the time, in experience, is rarely a simple date on the calendar; it

---

[12] It would extend my article overmuch to show how Paul dealt with slavery and male/female issues, for instance. But the glory of the gospel is that, by the Spirit, converted men and women, employers and employees, Jew and Gentile, educated and illiterate, could learn to live together in harmony. One of the great spin-offs of the new covenant, was it not?

[13] I would place this at the time of his death (Matt. 27:51; John 19:30), resurrection, culminating in the gift of the Spirit at Pentecost. As Gal. 5 (just one example) makes clear, the age of the new covenant is the age of the Spirit.

is a process, a time of transition, not a sudden, universal, total change or lurch overnight. Take the Norman Conquest of England. William defeated Harold at the Battle of Hastings (actually, at the Battle of Battle or Senlac) on 14th October 1066. That is an indisputable fact. From that day, England was no longer an independent Saxon kingdom, but had been reduced to a Norman colony, a vassal state; things were never going to be the same. The last Saxon king was dead; the first Norman monarch was about to be crowned. The feudal Saxon lords had been replaced by knights from Normandy. Saxon estates now belonged to a master race from over the Channel, the land would be covered in a series of massive castles serving as constant reminders of Norman superiority over the English, who were, from now on, virtual foreigners in what had been their own land.

The truth is, however, on the ground, out in the sticks, in the hamlets, along the hedgerows where the rustics – the ploughboys, carters, shepherds and cowmen – sat, chewing their midday victuals while chewing over (what seemed to them) the great events of the day,[14] things changed at snail pace; time was meted out in decades, lifetimes. The English were now a subjugated race, but Saxon ways, Saxon thinking, Saxon talk – Saxon England, itself – only gradually died, being only slowly replaced by Norman. (In fact, the two often amalgamated and became Anglo-Norman. This is one reason why the English

---

[14] Witness the conversations of the early-Victorian villagers (800 years after the Conquest) as perceptively and faithfully – not to say, amusingly – recorded by Thomas Hardy – surely the jewel in the crown of his prose work. Some earth-shattering event such as letting a side of bacon fall into the dust, or the flaring of a distant bonfire, being of far greater concern, and producing far more animation, than, say, any change in the government at Westminster. News of the grubbing up of an old apple tree triggered the amazed comment: 'Rooted? – you don't say it! Ah! stirring times we live in – stirring times' (Thomas Hardy: *Far From The Madding Crowd*). Politics, regime-change, and such-like to these worthies would have been as remote and unknowable as the stuff of outer space. How much more so in the years following 1066.

language is so rich). In one sense, then, in 1066 England was changed from a Saxon kingdom to a Norman colony. Overnight, on the calendar, simple, clear, cut and dried. But in reality, it was far more complicated, with many difficult, personal decisions to make.

Examples can be multiplied.[15]

On 9th November 1989 the Berlin Wall fell, but three and a half decades later and Europe (and the world) is still coming to terms with the consequences.[16]

On 31st January, 2020, at 23:00 GMT, the Brexit guillotine clanged down. Thump! But...[17]

Getting back to the supersession of the old covenant by the establishment of the new, the wonder is not that there was a time of actual transition in daily life, but that the change was accomplished at all, and accomplished, in the main, so relatively smoothly.[18] A lifetime of Jewish observance, sacrifice, priesthood, temple attendance, sacred Jewish dates and seasons – all abolished overnight? And, of course, it went far deeper

---

[15] Take the Roman Conquest of Britain, which led to the Romano-British period. Society at Bath wasn't suddenly, overnight, switched, like an electric light bulb, from Celtic-speaking, Iron-Age mystic barbarism, with its devotion to mysterious and ominous scooped-out heads, into a Latin-speaking Roman stateliness with its genteel 'taking of the waters' in the Great Bath of Minerva. Plenty of piping hot water had to flow from the spring before that happened! But, in part and substantially, that's what did happen! Even though the Icenian, Boudicca, or the Caledonian, Calgacus, to name but two, proved intransigent, Romano-Britain came into a settled-existence. Something similar applies to the decline of Romano-Britain. The books tell us that the Romans left Britain in 410. They did, and they did not! In some senses, they are still here!

[16] As I write (August 2023), the war still rages in Ukraine.

[17] That is, on 31st January, 2020 Britain left the European Union. Oh? As I write this (August 2023), things are still developing, painfully slowly at times.

[18] Consider the centuries of bitterness – the on-going legacy – of the slave trade from Africa to America. It is with us still.

than that. The culture of centuries was bred into the DNA of the Jews, and Jews had been born with old-covenant principles and practices (overloaded by layers of tradition) built into their genes, ingrained within their psyche.[19]

Moreover, it wasn't only the Jews who had to learn; converted pagans, too, had their world turned upside down. They, too, had to get to grips with 2 Corinthians 5:17. Anti-Semitism, for instance, didn't begin with the rise of Adolf Hitler in the 1920s.

All this potential for conflict was more than enough to torpedo the new covenant before the ship had left the wharf.

So, in those early post-Pentecost days, yes, of course, in Christ all the old-covenant Jewish practices had been fulfilled and were now rendered obsolete, over, finished, defunct. About this, there is no question. It happened at a stroke, But there is clear evidence that, in such cataclysmic circumstances as I have tried to spell out,[20] the apostolic writers were prepared to allow a certain amount of liberty to converted Jews to continue with such observances.[21] The same can be seen in the apostolic approach to the purchase and eating of meat from the shambles, meat which had been stamped in connection with idols (Acts

---

[19] I confess that despite all that I have written and preached, I still have puritan genes in my DNA.

[20] Such a sudden change must have been socially shattering. Try to imagine (for those of us living in the UK and US, for instance), if overnight, in one fell swoop, the UK and USA legal, social, religious and political systems were switched from Christendom convention to Sharia law. Think of the heap of personal problems a believer immediately would find piled on his plate, with no tradition to fall back on. Take marriage and family life, as just one example. And all in a virulent, hostile, unknown culture! Culture, singular? It's a miracle the early believers, starting so small and weak and insignificant, survived the onslaught of Jewish, Greek and Roman cultures in such intimidating circumstances, let alone grew in numbers to see the gospel expand into Europe! Who, in AD40, would have predicted that the *ekklēsia* would out-live the Roman Empire?

[21] Paul, himself, when necessary, took advantage of such liberty (Acts 16:3; 20:16; 21:17-26; 24:17).

15:29; 1 Cor. 8:4-13; 10:25-32; Tit. 1:15; Rev. 2:20). Liberty was allowed – but, as I say, liberty under with strict limits, and under certain, specified conditions.

All this balanced, sensitive fragility was, as I have said, put in jeopardy by the teaching and sinister design of those 'false brothers', the *pseudadelphoi*.[22]

I read Romans 14 and 15 in that light.

* * *

The point is this: some Jewish believers in the *ekklēsia* at Rome (Paul described them as 'weak' believers) felt that they should (or possibly could) hold on to some old-covenant ways, while other Jewish believers (Paul described them as 'strong' believers), and, of course, Gentile believers,[23] saw no reason to observe redundant old-covenant practices. In this potentially explosive atmosphere,[24] the eruption of the *pseudadelphoi* and their teaching posed a massive threat to the *ekklēsia*. In these highly-emotive circumstances, the apostles insisted that all concerned should calm down, and gently come to terms with their difference of opinion or conviction, doing so on the basis of their union with each other in Christ. Love, in the power of the Spirit, should conquer all. Only the love of Christ shed abroad in the heart (Rom. 5:5) can conquer prejudice. But it must. And it will (John 13:34-35; Jas. 2:1-13;1 John 4:19-21). Such was the spirit of the new age.

---

[22] All the arguments supporting these claims can be found in my works noted above. See in particular my *False*.

[23] Unless they had been infected by the *pseudadelphoi*.

[24] Witness the conflict between Protestants and Roman Catholics – with the police and the British Army writhing as a fated pig-in-the-middle – in Northern Ireland during 'The Troubles'. This thirty-year conflict over a political-religious issue, fuelled by ranters on both sides, cost more than 3500 lives, leaving countless others scarred – deeply scarred – physically or emotionally, or both, to this day; indeed, for life.

We need to be clear. When the apostle speaks of love, he does not mean 'warm sentiment'. Spiritual love goes hand in hand with knowledge, discernment, and such like; love does not mean ignorance, minimising real differences and scriptural distinctions, making things fudgy:

> It is my prayer that your love may abound more and more, with knowledge and all discernment, so that you may approve what is excellent, and so be pure and blameless for the day of Christ, filled with the fruit of righteousness that comes through Jesus Christ, to the glory and praise of God (Phil. 1:9-11).

As Paul told the Philippians:

> ...let your manner of life be worthy of the gospel of Christ, so that whether I come and see you or am absent, I may hear of you that you are standing firm in one spirit, with one mind striving side by side for the faith of the gospel, and not frightened in anything by your opponents (Phil. 1:27-28).

'Love' did not equate to 'give up thinking'.

And the end of this combination of spiritual love and knowledge is unity within the *ekklēsia*, unity in the truth, with every believer 'grow[ing] in the grace and knowledge of our Lord and Saviour Jesus Christ. To him be the glory both now and to the day of eternity. Amen' (2 Pet. 3:18).

To facilitate this process among converted Jews and Gentiles, as I have said, the apostles allowed, on a temporary, transitional basis, a measure of controlled and disciplined liberty for the observance of certain old-covenant practices. The upshot was that all believers ('weak' and 'strong') learned to live with each other in love and harmony, with a measure of give and take – but even then under strict conditions. The life the *ekklēsia* had not only to survive, but blossom, and do so in such delicate and highly-sensitive circumstances. *That is what Romans 14 and 15 is about.* It was designed to lead to the decaying and withering, and eventual dying out, of all the points of difference between believers, resulting, in due time, in a complete cessation of all old-covenant observance.[25]

Let me stress this vital point. Paul's teaching in Romans 14 and 15 concerns 'weak' and 'strong' believers. And it is self-evident that the apostolic aim was that the 'weak' should not stay weak but become strong – and thus bring the dispute to an end. That was the whole purpose of Paul's counsel. Remember that the dispute was fundamentally racially-motivated, strongly coloured by a doctrinal appreciation (or, more accurately, a lack of appreciation) about the change of covenants. The dispute would wither and die – not by heavy-handed legislation, but with the passage of time, and the maturing of the 'weak'. The time would come when very few would be left who had the slightest glimmer of what the dispute had been about. Compare the way in which the Puritan Sunday has morphed and virtually passed into oblivion in contemporary UK, not excepting evangelicals.

---

[25] Perhaps AD70 played its part in this.

# Christmas and Romans 14:5-6

Some believers think that Romans 14:5-6 warrants them holding special events to celebrate Christmas.[1] I wish to probe this claim.

Since I have already looked at Romans 14 and 15 in the round[2] – and it is vital to see the big picture in context – I now limit myself to quoting the two verses in question:

> One person esteems one day as better than another, while another esteems all days alike. Each one should be fully convinced in his own mind. The one who observes the day, observes it in honour of the Lord. The one who eats, eats in honour of the Lord, since he gives thanks to God, while the one who abstains, abstains in honour of the Lord and gives thanks to God (Rom. 14:5-6).

Let's state the obvious. And it is important not to miss the obvious. When he wrote to the Romans, the apostle couldn't have had any thought whatsoever of Christmas, since Christendom itself had not been invented, and it was only in the 9th century that Christendom really got a hold on Christmas. Let the *Encyclopaedia Britannica* explain:

> December 25 was first identified as the date of Jesus' birth by Sextus Julius Africanus in 221 and later became the universally accepted date... Christmas began to be widely celebrated with a specific liturgy in the 9th century.

So, whatever Paul was referring to in Romans 14, he was not referring to the observance of Christmas. No such date, season, festival in connection with Christ, existed at the time. No believer would have had a clue about any such observance. It is surely straining the limits of credulity to argue for Christmas on

---

[1] See, for example, Alan Hill: 'The Feast of Purim and the Feast of Christmas' (*Evangelical Times*, 26th Nov. 2021).

[2] My 'A Disaster Averted: Romans 14:5-6' (on my sermonaudio.com page) should be read before this article.

the basis of Romans 14: a case of having blatantly read the festival back into the passage and reading it out – eisegesis not exegesis – and showing determination and presumption by clinging to the pre-conceived idea.

Of course, Paul was talking about 'a day' – unspecified – so it is, I suppose, possible to read any day into the passage – the day of Christ's dipping by John in the Jordan, the day of his crucifixion, his burial, resurrection and ascension, for instance – if they can be determined, that is.[3] But why stop there? Why not take on board the entire Christendom calendar of holy days, festivals, and the like, and say that observing such dates and seasons is warranted?[4] And why not go further and embrace Valentine's Day, April Fool's Day, Mother's or Father's Day,[5] or whatever? Where to draw the line? Is there any line to be drawn?[6]

Or does it, in any case, smack of a deep-seated carnal desire for a return to the deluding tomfoolery of mystery plays, stained glass windows, incense and the like? And who is to call a halt – if a halt is to be called – and where? Shall we see 'The Jesus

---

[3] Christendom in what we now know as the British Isles had a long struggle over the date of Easter. Such things were – and still are – jam (with a hefty dollop of cream) for theologians, but it was the politicians who had to sort it out. As they duly did! 'The Synod of Whitby was... held in... 664, wherein King Oswiu ruled that his kingdom would calculate Easter and observe the monastic tonsure [haircut] according to the customs of Rome rather than the customs practiced by Irish monks at Iona and its satellite institutions' (Wikipedia). Theologians may pronounce, but ecclesiastical-politicians decide. Such is the way of Christendom.

[4] I have just checked 'Holy Days of Obligation 2023'. Quite a list!

[5] Indeed, it was at a Mothering-Day's Service in 1956 that I heard an Arminian preacher on Rev. 3:20. Nevertheless, God's blessing and use of any scheme, as we all well-know, does not signal his approval of every aspect of the performance; our warrant must be plain Scripture teaching.

[6] During the 1570s, when Elizabeth I cultivated the vision of herself as a goddess, the annual celebration of her Day of Accession outshone any remembrance of the old celebration-days when Rome held sway.

Jack-In-The-Green', 'The Jesus Mummers', 'The Jesus Morris Dancers', 'The Jesus Floral Dance', 'The Jesus Garden Fete and Cream Tea', 'The Jesus Hog Roast'?[7] Why not? All suitably sanctified by a having a special 'Christian Service' to mark The Event, all in the name of Jesus, of course! From time to time I see 'Pimms & Hymns' advertised locally in an Anglican church. Above all, think of The Opportunity for evangelism! Christmas, whatever else it is, above all is for evangelicals 'An Opportunity' – for what many evangelicals consider evangelism to be. And that, as I have tackled in several works, is fast becoming the virtual be-all-and-end-all for many evangelicals. So... on the matter of day-selection, when do we say enough is enough? I only ask – for the moment.

One thing we can be sure of; wherever we do draw the line, as noted above, theologians can always be relied on to come up with a theology to justify the wackiest of notions.[8]

But let me do more than ask or suggest: let me probe the way the passage from Romans has been used to try to justify Christmas observance. Use – or, abuse?

The first, the chief, thing to notice is that paying no attention to the big picture but just diving into the chapter and latching on to a few words is rather like plunging the hand into a barrel of sawdust in a fairground 'lucky dip' to see what you can come up with. The first step in applying Scripture must always be to make sure we are clear about the context. What is the big picture? As I have explained elsewhere,[9] ignoring the big picture, though it is commonly done, is not only shoddy; it is highly dangerous.

---

[7] Long-established English folklore customs, festivals and rites often with pagan connections. Traditional dressing up by the characters is typical. The 'Jack-in-the-Green', a dancing figure in a foliage-covered wicker shell, is often centre-stage in contemporary May Day celebrations. The Floral Dance celebrates the end of Winter and the start of Spring. And so on.
[8] Infant baptism is a classic. See my *Infant.*
[9] See my *False Brothers: Paul and Today.*

The fact is, treating the Bible as a barrel of bran strikes me as a case of: 'Have idea; find text!' It is not just the obvious point already made that the observance of Christmas could not have been in the apostle's mind when writing Romans 14 – it's not just a bare negative.[10] As so often, Paul wrote to deal with a specific problem. His solutions and explanations, of course, have far wider application, but the primary issue, the apostle's primary purpose in writing, must always play a leading part in any application we make of what he said.

As I have explained in an earlier article,[11] I have become convinced that the issue in Rome, that which Paul was dealing with in Romans 14 and 15 – and it was a thorny problem within the *ekklēsia* at Rome – was to do with some converted Jews, who even though they were living in the day of the new covenant, felt they ought to keep alive some of their familiar (and, no doubt, well-loved) Jewish customs, traditions, prohibitions, and the like, vestiges of the old, Mosaic covenant.[12] That was the issue at Rome. This must play a vital role in our understanding and application of the passage.

\* \* \*

Let me tease out some of the consequences of applying Romans 14 and 15 to Christmas observance. We need to think about who

---

[10] I recall that when I gave a paper to dismiss covenant-theology's claim of an Adamic covenant – 'the covenant of works' – an objector expressed her distaste by posting a blog comment to the effect that I showed the weakness of my argument when I observed that 'covenant' did not appear– as a word – in Gen. 2 & 3. In truth, that was by no means a major part of my argument, but merely a passing factual comment, an incidental. True, nevertheless.

[11] As already noted, see my 'A Disaster Averted: Romans 14:5-6' on my sermonaudio.com page. That article should be read to give the background to this article.

[12] Hebrews was written to prevent Jewish believers leaving Christ, leaving the new covenant, and returning to the old covenant. That, it surely does not need to be said, would have been a disaster of the first magnitude. See the warning passages in Hebrews (Heb. 2:1-4; 3:6 – 4:13; 5:11 – 6:12; 10:19-39; 12:3-29).

are the 'weak', and who are the 'strong'. Clearly the 'weak' must be believers who would like to have Christmas in *ekklēsia* life, whereas the 'strong' must be believers who would not. Take this a bit further: supposing, for sake of argument, that Paul's words *can* be applied to Christmas, it would mean that believers who do not want Christmas would tolerate it for the sake of those who do, but only on the clear understanding that this state of affairs was temporary until the 'weak' came to see that the festival should be stopped.

Is this how present-day evangelicals see Christmas? Is this the reason for having a Christmas Event – so that any superstitious clinging on to Christmas by some believers might gradually wither and die? That's the last thing most Christmas-advocates would want. Christmas has been invented. It has been part of the scenery for countless generations – indeed, for more than 1000 years. It has grown in importance. We like it. We can't imagine life without it. It is here to stay. To (lightly, but only lightly) accommodate scripture:

> An appalling and horrible thing has happened in the [churches] [they set up Christmas Events]; [and] my people love to have it so, but what will you do when the end comes? (Jer. 5:30-31).

Again, the observances Paul spoke of in Romans 14 and 15, I suggest, almost certainly had some kind of scriptural warrant somewhere in the background. After all, old-covenant practices were right and proper – *in the days of the old covenant!* What scriptural warrant is there for the Christmas festival? It's basis is pagan!

And don't the following scripture passages rebuke any tendency to take pagan concepts and 'Christendomise' them?

> [As God commanded his old-covenant people:] Learn not the way of the nations [pagans] nor be dismayed at the signs of the heavens because the nations are dismayed at them, for the customs of the peoples are vanity (Jer. 10:2-3).

> This people honours me with their lips, but their heart is far from me; in vain do they worship me, teaching as doctrines the commandments of men (Matt. 15:8-9).

145

[As God commands his new-covenant people:] Formerly, when you did not know God, you were enslaved to those that by nature are not gods. But now that you have come to know God, or rather to be known by God, how can you turn back again to the weak and worthless elementary principles of the world, whose slaves you want to be once more? You observe days and months and seasons and years! I am afraid I may have laboured over you in vain (Gal. 4:8-11).

[Again:] See to it that no one takes you captive by philosophy and empty deceit, according to human tradition, according to the elemental spirits [principles] of the world, and not according to Christ (Col. 2:8).[13]

So much for my revisiting Romans 14:5-6 in connection with claims about Christmas. I remain convinced that those two verses really do not support its observance. And that – if you have not already worked it out – is a bit of an understatement!

---

[13] Incidentally, Christ's strong rebuke in Rev. 2:20 seems to me to have within it some relevance to the observance of Christmas. The problem at Thyatira, it would appear, was eating idol-offered meat in connection with pagan festivals – not a million miles from current observance of Christmas, especially if we substitute 'religious-superstition' for 'idol-offered'.

# Purim and Christmas

Some believers claim that the Esther account of the Jewish institution of an annual feast to celebrate their deliverance from the evil machinations of Haman gives them the warrant to set up special events to celebrate Christmas.[1] I wish to probe this claim.

The Jews certainly experienced a most remarkable, sovereign deliverance by God from Haman's vile schemes, and, wishing to preserve a sense of perpetual gratitude to God in all following generations of Jews, they established an annual celebration of the event – Purim. This is beyond dispute. As the relevant passage in Esther tells us:

> Mordecai recorded these things [that is, the deliverance] and sent letters to all the Jews who were in all the provinces of King Ahasuerus, both near and far, obliging them to keep the fourteenth day of the month Adar and also the fifteenth day of the same, year by year, as the days on which the Jews got relief from their enemies, and as the month that had been turned for them from sorrow into gladness and from mourning into a holiday; that they should make them days of feasting and gladness, days for sending gifts of food to one another and gifts to the poor.
> So the Jews accepted what they had started to do, and what Mordecai had written to them. For Haman the Agagite, the son of Hammedatha, the enemy of all the Jews, had plotted against the Jews to destroy them, and had cast Pur (that is, cast lots), to crush and to destroy them. But when it came before the king, he gave orders in writing that his evil plan that he had devised against the Jews should return on his own head, and that he and his sons should be hanged on the gallows. Therefore they called these days Purim, after the term Pur. Therefore, because of all that was written in this letter, and of what they had faced in this matter, and of what had happened to them, the Jews firmly obligated themselves and their offspring and all who

---

[1] See, for example, Alan Hill: 'The Feast of Purim and the Feast of Christmas' (*Evangelical Times*, 26th Nov. 2021).

joined them, that without fail they would keep these two days according to what was written and at the time appointed every year, that these days should be remembered and kept throughout every generation, in every clan, province, and city, and that these days of Purim should never fall into disuse among the Jews, nor should the commemoration of these days cease among their descendants.
Then Queen Esther, the daughter of Abihail, and Mordecai the Jew gave full written authority, confirming this second letter about Purim. Letters were sent to all the Jews, to the 127 provinces of the kingdom of Ahasuerus, in words of peace and truth, that these days of Purim should be observed at their appointed seasons, as Mordecai the Jew and Queen Esther obligated them, and as they had obligated themselves and their offspring, with regard to their fasts and their lamenting. The command of Esther confirmed these practices of Purim, and it was recorded in writing (Esth. 9:20-32).

God did not institute this annual feast of Purim; it was Mordecai's idea, and it was confirmed by Queen Esther. But God nowhere rebuked the Jews for what they did. And, of course, the whole episode is set out in Scripture. Naturally, therefore, it really does appear that the Jews were perfectly in order to set up this annual celebration feast of remembrance. And I can see how easy it is to move from that to say that believers can do something similar today. It seems but a little step from the Jewish institution and annual observance of Purim, to Christendom and the observance of Christmas.

But shouldn't we pause and ask a few questions before we jump? Even the world knows that we are well-advised to look before we leap, not leap then look. Alas, of course, as far as Christmas goes, Christendom long ago leapt in. Talk about spilt milk and bottles!

This leap from Purim to Christmas smacks – to me, at least – of the frequent mistake evangelicals make when they move blithely from the old to new covenant; namely, in their bland confidence, they either conveniently forget or ignore – or is it that they are ignorant of? – the plain, indisputable fact that because Christ has fulfilled the old covenant, rendered it obsolete, and brought in the new,[2] there is a gaping discontinuity between the two Testaments. For whatever reason, this massive discontinuity often goes out of the window. Of course, I recognise that – in accordance with Romans 15:4; 1 Corinthians 5:6-8; 6:19; 9:1-18; 10:1-33; 14:20-22 and Hebrews, for instance – the new covenant does frequently draw on the old covenant to find spiritual instruction for believers, and it undoubtedly gives us warrant to do the same – *but it must be done with due care, and be properly nuanced.*[3] I further note, that, in accordance with those passages just cited, this use of the old covenant is not so that believers can copy an old-covenant practice, or on that basis set up something new in the life of the *ekklēsia*. Indeed, as it seems to me at least, new-covenant references to the old covenant often wear the mantle of warnings, warnings as to what should be avoided by believers, warnings as to the consequences of disobedience to plain new-covenant instruction. The classic statement must be:

> All Scripture[4] is breathed out by God and profitable for teaching, for reproof, for correction, and for training in righteousness, that the man of God may be complete, equipped for every good work (2 Tim. 3:16-17).

I am convinced that none of this should be treated lightly; it must not be brushed aside, ignored. What I am saying is this: when believers turn to the old covenant, they should always – always – keep firmly in mind this big – massive – picture of the change of covenants, and the consequences of the discontinuity thereby introduced. This, alas, is far from always being the case. And that's putting it mildly! What's more, the consequences of

---

[2] See many of my works, including *Christ Is All*; 'A Disaster Averted: Romans 14:5-6' on my sermonaudio.com page.
[3] See, for instance, my 'Separation Essential: No Mixture! Deut. 22:9-11' on my sermonaudio.com page.
[4] By the time Paul wrote this letter, some parts of what would become the New Testament were coming into use, but 'all Scripture' would still be mainly the Old Testament, primarily the Septuagint.

ignoring the covenant-discontinuity introduced by Christ are far from trivial.[5]

Incidentally, is it not significant that Christ promised that the Spirit would lead the apostles – not the Fathers, not the Christendom engineers, but the apostles – into all – not some, not most, but all – truth? He most certainly did:

> I will ask the Father, and he will give you another Helper, to be with you forever, even the Spirit of truth, whom the world cannot receive, because it neither sees him nor knows him. You know him, for he dwells with you and will be in you... The Helper, the Holy Spirit, whom the Father will send in my name, he will teach you all things and bring to your remembrance all that I have said to you...

I break in to highlight Christ's promise, Christ's categorical assurance, by stressing his own specific, clear limit or condition: 'The Holy Spirit... will teach you all things and bring to your remembrance all that I have said to you'. On the basis of Christ's words, is it not fair to say that whatever the apostles might later claim, whatever they might lay out as definitive truth, must have some connection – however tenuous, fleeting or flimsy (for fairness in argument, I am stretching this piece of elastic to breaking point) – with the plain teaching of the Master? 'All that I have said to you' certainly implies as much. Let me hasten to add – if it is not clear by what I have said – that I am persuaded that the condition is far more rigorous than I have allowed.

Christ went on:

---

[5] As a case in point, look at the way the Reformed so-called 'threefold division of the law' allows them to play fast and loose with the old covenant to make it fit into their system of theology. And with devastating results. See my series *New-Covenant Articles* for examples.

Again, those who sing only psalms must have some awkward moments – unless they take full account of the covenantal discontinuity (see, for instance, Ps. 18:20-24; 69:22-28; 109:6-15; 137:8-9; 139:19-22; 150:1-6).

When the Helper comes, whom I will send to you from the Father, the Spirit of truth, who proceeds from the Father, he will bear witness about me. And you also will bear witness, because you have been with me from the beginning...

I break in again. Christ was not making a pedantic point about dates: 'You have been with me since 1st October', or whatever. Far from it. 'You have been with from the start; you have seen, you have heard, you have witnessed every aspect of my ministry and teaching. Make sure what you teach, what you set up, bears unmistakable evidence of being strictly in line with what you have seen in me'. It cannot be denied that that is what Christ's words amount to. Here again we have a clear link between the teaching of the apostles and the teaching of Christ.

Christ continued:

I tell you the truth: it is to your advantage that I go away, for if I do not go away, the Helper will not come to you. But if I go, I will send him to you. And when he comes, he will convict the world concerning sin and righteousness and judgment: concerning sin, because they do not believe in me; concerning righteousness, because I go to the Father, and you will see me no longer; concerning judgment, because the ruler of this world is judged.
I still have many things to say to you, but you cannot bear them now. When the Spirit of truth comes, he will guide you into all the truth, for he will not speak on his own authority, but whatever he hears he will speak, and he will declare to you the things that are to come. He will glorify me, for he will take what is mine and declare it to you. All that the Father has is mine; therefore I said that he will take what is mine and declare it to you (John 14:16-26; 15:26-27; 16:7-15).

I quite understand, of course, that if, like Roman Catholics, one believes that this means that the Church (however it may be defined) is here given warrant to develop truth in accordance with a claimed-revelation from the Spirit through popes, councils, moderators, bishops, pastors, committees, conferences, or whatever, then Christendom has been handed a blank cheque, made out to 'cash'. Which too often just about sums up the present state of affairs! But think! What happens when Church

'A' says the bread in the Lord's supper becomes the actual body of Christ, and Church 'B' says that it does not...? That's just one example. Which Church are we talking about?[6] And what do we do when a Church changes its mind?[7]

If, however, you are convinced that the cumulative weight of the above Scripture passages leaves no room for the slightest doubt, but that Christ promised that the apostles, by the Spirit, would deliver his final and definitive word to his people for this entire age – and that is my position – your feet are fixed on very different ground. The first ground is shifting sand, at the changing whim of men; the second is solid rock, granite, immoveable.

The consequence is clear: whoever devises any scheme, any scheme whatsoever, on whatever specious ground, if it is not absolutely in accord with the apostolic revelation, that teaching must be rejected, refused, and treated as a defection from 'the faith [the system, the gospel] that was once for all delivered to the saints' by the Spirit through the apostles (Jude 3). Instead of compromising that 'faith' – compromising it by accommodating it to pagan ideas, playing with 'the faith', tinkering with it, adding to it – we have 'to contend for' it (Jude 3), even 'earnestly contend' for it.[8] 'Contending for the faith' cannot easily be understood as 'add bits and pieces to it as you wish', or 'pull it into any shape you think fit'.

This is no idle, academic debate, a pleasant diversion for the fun of it. The least straying from the gospel is straying, and taking that slippery path has every prospect of being fatal.[9] To tinker with the apostolic revelation is nothing short of sin. It has the

---

[6] When Cyprian (echoed by Calvin) said there is no salvation outside the Church, which Church did he (and Calvin) mean? And which is it today?

[7] Church Councils have been contradicted by later Councils. One pope has contradicted another.

[8] The preposition, *epi*, in *epagōnizomai*, is intensive.

[9] See my *False Brothers: Paul and Today*.

smack of the 'itching ears' so much disliked by Paul (2 Tim. 4:1-5).

Moreover, whereas the Jews set up their feast of Purim from scratch, off their own bat, so to speak, when it came to Christmas, Christendom went to a pagan festival, adapted and adopted it to form their 'custom'. For this reason alone, to claim that Christendom is warranted to argue on the basis of the Jews' behaviour over Purim seems to me to be, at the very least, doubtful; the link seems tenuous, and the leap a large one over a yawning gap. Christmas was entirely a pagan mid-winter festival which, as is Christendom's wont, Christendom found, liked, adapted – 'Christendomised', is the proper word – and adopted to become a major Christendom festival, heavily laced – overloaded – with pagan excess. Is it fair, therefore, to link Purim and Christmas? Is it right?

The believers' observance of Christmas is not remotely as a result of a scriptural command or new-covenant practice. Indeed, it is a custom, tradition, invented by Christendom, pure and simple. Let's not kid ourselves. Christmas, fundamentally, has nothing to do with the Bible – in particular, the teaching of Christ or the apostles – but everything to do with the machinations of Christendom's political and philosophical engineers and managers. Those clever gentlemen invented Christmas[10] when they 'Christendomised' the pagan Saturnalia; that is the unvarnished truth, pure and simple. Having done that, the theologians had to get to work, hunting for some sort of scriptural – or, rather, theological, philosophical – justification for the new idea. As always, they found a way.[11]

In any case, were the Jews to be commended for setting up this annual commemoration? This is always assumed: but on what grounds? Because it is recorded in Scripture? If so, that opens the door to any amount of abuse!

---

[10] When did Christendom start to call on Purim for justification? In my *Infant*, I showed that the infant-baptism use of Christ and the children (Mark 10:13-16) to justify their practice was a very late development.
[11] Infant baptism is a classic. See my *Infant*.

Again, did Christ observe Purim in his day? I know of no written evidence which shows that he did. I don't say that he did not; I just don't know.[12]

The implication is that although they had no command from God, the Jews were perfectly right to establish such a feast. But playing with a knife is a risky pastime. It could, with equal weight, be said: 'It is significant that there is no commendation from God for this addition of a feast day to the Jewish calendar'; that is to say, the Jews were acting out of order. I don't see that the reference to Purim takes us any further. True enough, Scripture tells us what the Jews did, but I know of no scripture which commends them for what they did.

Moreover, Scripture is full of such things.

Sometimes, God intervened to set up memorials (Num. 16:36-40; Josh. 4:1-7,19-24, for instance). But not with Purim!

Sometimes, events just happened.

Joshua accepted the Gibeonite lies, and Israel had to live with the painful consequences (Josh. 9:1-16; 2 Sam. 21:1). Scripture records it. Why? As something for us to adapt and use for our purposes? Or does it serve as a warning?

The Eastern tribes built an altar of witness and the Western tribes accepted it (Josh. 22:10-34). All the ramifications of the episode are recorded – but for our emulation? Or what?

Israel preserved the bronze serpent of the wilderness by which, under God's command, promise and power, many were delivered during a time of widespread death by poisonous snakes (Num. 21:4-9) – Nehushtan. They not only preserved the

---

[12] Take Hannukah (the Feast of Dedication). This annual festival was established in the inter-testamental period when the Maccabees re-dedicated the temple after its desecration by Antiochus Epiphanes. We know that 'the Feast of Dedication took place at Jerusalem. It was winter, and Jesus was walking in the temple, in the colonnade of Solomon' (John 10:22-23). But did he observe the feast? What lesson should we draw?

artefact; they even worshipped it – until Hezekiah stepped in and destroyed it (2 Kings 18:4). Which aspect of that episode should believers follow – if any? Christ used the actual deliverance to speak of the gospel:

> As Moses lifted up the serpent in the wilderness, so must the Son of Man be lifted up, that whoever believes in him may have eternal life (John 3:14-15).

But was Christ putting his seal of approval on the subsequent way the Jews behaved over the brass serpent? Of course he wasn't!

Israel desired to have a king to be like the pagans (Deut. 17:14-20; 28:36; 1 Sam. 8:19-22) – which led to the Davidic dynasty. How should we apply this today? Were the Israelites right to want to ape the pagans? Of course not. Such behaviour was forbidden countless times by Moses and the prophets.[13] Yet God made major use of the concept of the kingdom. The question is: how are we to interpret and apply Israel's desire? Let's have a pope! What a good idea! Save us all the trouble of thinking for ourselves – just listen to the talking head! Get it straight from the horse's mouth – even though the latest horse might contradict a previous occupant of the stable. Really?

David dedicated pagan gold and bronze to God's use (2 Sam. 8:11; 1 Chron. 18:8-11). He took a jewel from the pagan's crown to add to his own royal gems (2 Sam. 12:30). What application – if any – should we make of this today? Should we follow this practice in the *ekklēsia*?

David erected a separate tent – apart from the tabernacle, and in Jerusalem not Gibeon – in which to house the ark of the covenant (2 Chron. 1:3-6), until Solomon reunited both tents in the newly-constructed temple (2 Chron. 5:2-14). Yet Moses had been commanded to erect the tabernacle (with its inner tent) precisely as God commanded him (Heb. 8:5). Was David right? Is this erection of a second tent recorded so that we might act in

---

[13] See my *Evangelicals Warned*.

155

a similar way, and make changes over dipping or the supper, for instance?

Something similar can be said of the new rules for the priests and levites introduced by David and Solomon, enforced by Josiah (2 Chron. 35:4-6). And what about Jeremiah's lament for Josiah (2 Chron. 35:25)?

Think of James' odd behaviour and Paul's acceptance of it (Acts 21).[14]

Think of Paul's appeal to Rome (Acts 25:10-11) and all the consequences. Good? Bad? Indifferent?

And so on.

Are these recorded simply as facts, warnings or role models? And if the latter, do they give us a blank cheque to set up any observance, practice or ritual that we like?

Indeed, while the parallel, I admit, is not exact, surely there is at least a whiff of a hint of warning in the shenanigans of Jeroboam son of Nebat. I refer, of course, to these events:

> Jeroboam built Shechem in the hill country of Ephraim and lived there. And he went out from there and built Penuel. And Jeroboam said in his heart: 'Now the kingdom will turn back to the house of David. If this people go up to offer sacrifices in the temple of the LORD at Jerusalem, then the heart of this people will turn again to their lord, to Rehoboam king of Judah, and they will kill me and return to Rehoboam king of Judah'. So the king took counsel and made two calves of gold. And he said to the people: 'You have gone up to Jerusalem long enough. Behold your gods, O Israel, who brought you up out of the land of Egypt'. And he set one in Bethel, and the other he put in Dan. Then this thing became a sin, for the people went as far as Dan to be before one. He also made temples on high places and appointed priests from among all the people, who were not of the levites. And Jeroboam

---

[14] See my 'Does Acts 21 Confirm Sabbath Keeping for Believers?' in my *New-Covenant Articles Volume Eleven*. James, unwittingly or not, played his part in the débacle over the law at Antioch (Gal. 2:11-14).

appointed a feast on the fifteenth day of the eighth month like the feast that was in Judah, and he offered sacrifices on the altar. So he did in Bethel, sacrificing to the calves that he made. And he placed in Bethel the priests of the high places that he had made. He went up to the altar that he had made in Bethel on the fifteenth day in the eighth month, in the month that he had devised from his own heart. And he instituted a feast for the people of Israel and went up to the altar to make offerings.

And behold, a man of God came out of Judah by the word of the LORD to Bethel. Jeroboam was standing by the altar to make offerings. And the man cried against the altar by the word of the LORD and said: 'O altar, altar, thus says the LORD: "Behold, a son shall be born to the house of David, Josiah by name, and he shall sacrifice on you the priests of the high places who make offerings on you, and human bones shall be burned on you"'. And he gave a sign the same day, saying: 'This is the sign that the LORD has spoken: "Behold, the altar shall be torn down, and the ashes that are on it shall be poured out"'. And when the king heard the saying of the man of God, which he cried against the altar at Bethel, Jeroboam stretched out his hand from the altar, saying: 'Seize him'. And his hand, which he stretched out against him, dried up, so that he could not draw it back to himself. The altar also was torn down, and the ashes poured out from the altar, according to the sign that the man of God had given by the word of the LORD (1 Kings 12:25-33; 13:1-5).

Following the strange affair of the intervention of 'an old prophet [who] lived in Bethel', which led to the death of the original 'man of God' by a lion (1 Kings 13:11-31), the 'old prophet' prophesied that...

...the saying that [the man of God] called out by the word of the LORD against the altar in Bethel and against all the houses of the high places that are in the cities of Samaria shall surely come to pass (1 Kings 13:32).

The upshot? Just this:

After this thing Jeroboam did not turn from his evil way, but made priests for the high places again from among all the people. Any who would, he ordained to be priests of the high places. And this thing became sin to the house of Jeroboam, so as to cut it off and to destroy it from the face of the earth (1 Kings 13:33-34).

Something to take onboard, in the present discussion, don't you think?

Moreover, the actual Jewish Purim-celebration, as much as I have witnessed it, provides a signally bad role model for believers – overt, crude hatred which smacks of a kind of reversed Nazi-rejoicing over the Jewish genocide and barbarity, is my impression – Jewish hilarity at the wholesale slaughter of pagans. Mordecai and Esther might well think again if they knew that in making Purim a Jewish obligation, later generations would re-engineer it into a virtual obligation for carnality.

It goes without saying that it is always dangerous to argue from silence, but if Christmas (and Easter) celebration, and the like, is such a good thing for believers, is it not odd that neither Christ or any apostle instituted it – especially while remembering that Christ did institute dipping and the Supper. This takes us back to the question of authority. Christmas: is it Scripture or Saturnalia? The foolishness and carnality of Christmas bespeak its origin.

\* \* \*

In light of all the above concerning Purim, is Christendom warranted to adopt the pagan mid-winter festival and turn it into a major event in the 'Christian' calendar?

I know my answer. Reader, what's yours?

# Reformed Infant Baptismal Regeneration

The Roman Catholic Church, Lutherans[1] and the Church of England hold that a minister sprinkling babies and using the right formula regenerates those infants. But what about the Reformed who baptise infants? What do they believe? What follows is self-evident. The statements – which are just a sample of what might be gathered – are riddled with Christendom-speak, brought about by the mixing of the two covenants, the old and the new. I refer to such things as talk of Israel and the *ekklēsia* as two aspects of one church, talk of the visible church, sacraments, with baptism – sprinkling – as a seal. And, it must be borne in mind, the use of 'seal' means guarantee, assurance. What is more, the double-speaking metaphysics of the theologians must not divert attention from reality: it is not what the ivory-towered Reformed theologians and the officiating minister pronounce but what the people standing at the font believe, what they instinctively feel and what they hope for. About that there is no question. Most of them believe, feel, hope that the baby is now safe; something has been done to him or her. Phew, that's a relief! Whatever happens from now on, the child is in the covenant, whatever that may mean. And the growing child is constantly reminded that he or she is in the covenant. That's the stark reality.

The business is a diabolical delusion from start to finish, based on confusion of the two covenants old and new.

So to business. Judge for yourself. I will not comment or correct the mistaken theology in what follows, having already fully dealt with all the issues.[2]

---

[1] See my *Luther on Baptism*.
[2] See my *Infant*.

## The Heidelberg Catechism

69. Q. How does holy baptism signify and seal to you that the one sacrifice of Christ on the cross benefits you?
A. In this way: Christ instituted this outward washing and with it gave the promise that, as surely as water washes away the dirt from the body, so certainly his blood and Spirit wash away the impurity of my soul, that is, all my sins.
70. Q. What does it mean to be washed with Christ's blood and Spirit?
A. To be washed with Christ's blood means to receive forgiveness of sins from God, through grace, because of Christ's blood, poured out for us in his sacrifice on the cross. To be washed with his Spirit means to be renewed by the Holy Spirit and sanctified to be members of Christ, so that more and more we become dead to sin and lead a holy and blameless life... Scripture calls baptism the washing of rebirth and the washing away of sins...
72. Q. Does this outward washing with water itself wash away sins?
A. No, only the blood of Jesus Christ and the Holy Spirit cleanse us from all sins.
73. Q. Why then does the Holy Spirit call baptism the washing of regeneration and the washing away of sins?
A. God speaks in this way for a good reason. He wants to teach us that the blood and Spirit of Christ remove our sins just as water takes away dirt from the body. But, even more important, he wants to assure us by this divine pledge and sign that we are as truly cleansed from our sins spiritually as we are bodily washed with water.
74. Q. Should infants, too, be baptised?
A. Yes. Infants as well as adults belong to God's covenant and congregation. Through Christ's blood the redemption from sin and the Holy Spirit, who works faith, are promised to them no less than to adults. Therefore, by baptism, as the sign of the covenant, they must be incorporated into the Christian church and distinguished from the children of unbelievers. This was done in the old covenant by circumcision, in place of which baptism was instituted in the new covenant...

## John Calvin:

Just as circumcision, which was a kind of badge to the Jews, assuring them that they were adopted as the people and family of God... while they, in their turn, professed their allegiance to God, so now we are initiated by baptism, so as to be enrolled among his people, and at the same time swear unto his name. Hence it is incontrovertible that baptism has been substituted for circumcision, and performs the same office. Now, if we are to investigate whether or not baptism is justly given to infants, will we not say that the man trifles, or rather is delirious, who would stop short at the element of water, and the external observance, and not allow his mind to rise to the spiritual mystery? If reason is listened to, it will undoubtedly appear that baptism is properly administered to infants as a thing due to them. The Lord did not anciently bestow circumcision upon them without making them partakers of all the things signified by circumcision. He would have deluded his people with mere imposture, had he quieted them with fallacious symbols: the very idea is shocking. He distinctly declares that the circumcision of the infant will be instead of a seal of the promise of the covenant. But if the covenant remains firm and fixed, it is no less applicable to the children of Christians in the present day, than to the children of the Jews under the Old Testament. Now, if they are partakers of the thing signified, how can they be denied the sign? If they obtain the reality, how can they be refused the figure? The external sign is so united in the sacrament with the word, that it cannot be separated from it.[3]

Baptism... is given as a pledge of our adoption; for by it we are grafted into the body of Christ, so as to be washed and cleansed by his blood, and then renewed in purity of life by his Holy Spirit... As God receives little children into the Church with their fathers, we say, upon the authority of Jesus Christ, that the children of believing parents should be baptised.[4]

## The Belgic Confession:

We believe that every man who is earnestly studious of obtaining life eternal ought to be but once baptised with this only baptism, without ever repeating the same, since we cannot be born twice. Neither doth this baptism only avail us at the time when the water is poured upon us and received by us, but

---

[3] John Calvin *Institutes of the Christian Religion* 4.16.4-5.
[4] John Calvin: The French Confession of Faith, 1559, XXXV.

also through the whole course of our life. Therefore we detest the error of the Anabaptists, who... condemn the baptism of the infants of believers, whom we believe ought to be baptised and sealed with the sign of the covenant, as the children in Israel formerly were circumcised upon the same promises which are made unto our children. And indeed, Christ shed his blood no less for the washing of the children of the faithful than for adult persons; and therefore, they ought to receive the sign and sacrament of that which Christ has done for them; as the Lord commanded in the law, that they should be made partakers of the sacrament of Christ's suffering and death shortly after they were born, by offering for them a lamb, which was a sacrament of Jesus Christ. Moreover, what circumcision was to the Jews, that baptism is to our children.[5]

## The Scots Confession:

We utterly condemn the vanity of those who affirm the sacraments to be nothing else than naked and bare signs. No, we assuredly believe that by baptism we are engrafted into Christ Jesus, to be made partakers of his righteousness, by which our sins are covered and remitted.[6]

## Canons of the Synod of Dort:

The children of believers are holy, not by nature, but in virtue of the covenant of grace, in which they, together with the parents, are comprehended; godly parents have no reason to doubt of the election and salvation of their children whom it pleases God to call out of this life in their infancy.[7]

## The Westminster Confession:

Baptism is a sacrament of the New Testament, ordained by Jesus Christ, not only for the solemn admission of the party baptised into the visible Church; but also, to be unto him a sign and seal of the covenant of grace, of his ingrafting into Christ, of regeneration, of remission of sins, and of his giving up unto God through Jesus Christ, to walk in the newness of life... Not

---

[5] Article 34.
[6] Chapter 21.
[7] Of Divine Predestination, Article 17.

only those that do actually profess faith in and obedience unto Christ, but also the infants of one or both believing parents, are to be baptised... Although it be a great sin to contemn or neglect this ordinance, yet grace and salvation are not so inseparably annexed unto it, as that no person can be regenerated or saved without it; or, that all that are baptised are undoubtedly regenerated... The efficacy of baptism is not tied to that moment of time wherein it is administered; yet notwithstanding, by the right use of this ordinance, the grace promised is not only offered, but really exhibited and conferred, by the Holy Ghost, to such (whether of age or infants) as that grace belongs unto, according to the counsel of God's own will, in his appointed time.[8]

## The Westminster Larger Catechism:

Q. 165. What is baptism?

A. Baptism is a sacrament of the New Testament, wherein Christ has ordained the washing with water in the name of the Father, and of the Son, and of the Holy Ghost, to be a sign and seal of ingrafting into himself, of remission of sins by his blood, and regeneration by his Spirit; of adoption, and resurrection unto everlasting life; and whereby the parties baptised are solemnly admitted into the visible church, and enter into an open and professed engagement to be wholly and only the Lord's.

Q. 166. Unto whom is baptism to be administered?

A. Baptism is not to be administered to any that are out of the visible church, and so strangers from the covenant of promise, till they profess their faith in Christ, and obedience to him, but infants descending from parents, either both, or but one of them, professing faith in Christ, and obedience to him, are in that respect within the covenant, and to be baptised.

Q. 167. How is our baptism to be improved by us?

A. ...by serious and thankful consideration of the nature of it, and of the ends for which Christ instituted it, the privileges and benefits conferred and sealed thereby... by growing up to assurance of pardon of sin, and of all other blessings sealed to us in that sacrament; by drawing strength from the death and resurrection of Christ, into whom we are baptised...

---

[8] Chapter XXVIII. 1,4,5,6.

## The Westminster Shorter Catechism:

Q. 94. What is baptism?

A. Baptism is a sacrament, wherein the washing with water in the name of the Father, and of the Son, and of the Holy Ghost, signifies and seals our ingrafting into Christ, and partaking of the benefits of the covenant of grace...

Q. 95. To whom is baptism to be administered?

A. Baptism is not to be administered to any that are out of the visible church, till they profess their faith in Christ, and obedience to him; but the infants of such as are members of the visible church are to be baptised.

## The Westminster Directory of Public Worship:

The Lord Jesus Christ instituted baptism as a covenant sign and seal for his church. He uses it not only for the solemn admission of the person who is baptised into the visible church, but also to depict and to confirm his ingrafting of that person into himself and his including that person in the covenant of grace.

The Lord uses baptism to portray to us that we and our children are conceived and born in sin and need to be cleansed.

He uses it to witness and seal to us the remission of sins and the bestowal of all the gifts of salvation through union with Christ. Baptism with water signifies and seals cleansing from sin by the blood and the Spirit of Christ, together with our death unto sin and our resurrection unto newness of life by virtue of the death and resurrection of Christ. The time of the outward application of the sign does not necessarily coincide with the inward work of the Holy Spirit which the sign represents and seals to us. Because these gifts of salvation are the gracious provision of the triune God, who is pleased to claim us as his very own, we are baptised into the name of the Father and of the Son and of the Holy Spirit.

In our baptism, the Lord puts his name on us, claims us as his own, and summons us to assume the obligations of the covenant. He calls us to believe in Jesus Christ as our Saviour, to renounce the devil, the world, and the flesh, and to walk humbly with our God in devotion to his commandments...

Although our young children do not yet understand these things, they are nevertheless to be baptised. For God commands that all who are under his covenant of grace be given the sign of the covenant.

God made the promise of the covenant to believers and to their offspring. In the Old Testament, he declared to Abraham: 'And I will establish my covenant between me and you and your seed after you in their generations for an everlasting covenant, to be a God unto you, and to your seed after you' (Gen. 17:7). For this reason, in the Old Testament, God commanded that covenant infants be given the sign of circumcision.

The covenant is the same in essence in both the Old and the New Testaments. Indeed, the grace of God for the consolation of believers is even more fully manifested in the New Testament. Thus, rather than rescinding the covenant promise to believers and to their offspring in the New Testament, God reaffirms it. He declares that 'the promise is unto you, and to your children' (Acts 2:39). He promises: 'Believe on the Lord Jesus Christ, and you will be saved, and your house' (Acts 16:31). He affirms that if even one parent is a believer, the children are 'holy' (1 Cor. 7:14). Moreover, our Saviour admitted little children into his presence, embracing and blessing them, and saying: 'Of such is the kingdom of God' (Mark 10:14).

And so, in the New Testament no less than in the Old, the children of believers have an interest in the covenant and a right to the covenant sign and to the outward privileges of the covenant people, the church. In the New Testament, baptism has replaced circumcision as the covenant sign. Therefore, by the covenant sign of baptism the children of believers are to be distinguished from the world and solemnly admitted into the visible church...

The minister shall then pray for the presence and blessing of the triune God, that the grace signified and sealed by baptism may be abundantly realised...

The Lord Jesus Christ instituted baptism as a covenant sign and seal for his church. He uses it not only for the solemn admission of the person who is baptised into the visible church, but also to depict and to confirm his ingrafting of that person into himself and his including that person in the covenant of grace.

The Lord uses baptism to portray to us that we and our children are conceived and born in sin and need to be cleansed.

He uses it to witness and seal to us the remission of sins and the bestowal of all the gifts of salvation through union with Christ. Baptism with water signifies and seals cleansing from sin by the blood and the Spirit of Christ, together with our death unto sin and our resurrection unto newness of life by virtue of the death and resurrection of Christ. Because these gifts of salvation are the gracious provision of the triune God, who is pleased to claim us as his very own, we are baptised into the name of the Father and of the Son and of the Holy Spirit.

In our baptism, the Lord puts his name on us, claims us as his own, and summons us to assume the obligations of the covenant. He calls us to believe in Jesus Christ as our Saviour, to renounce the devil, the world, and the flesh, and to walk humbly with our God in devotion to his commandments.

## The Second Helvetic Confession:

...by baptism we are ingrafted into the body of Christ... But now since Christ the true Messiah is exhibited unto us, and the abundance of grace is poured forth upon the people of the New Testament, the sacraments of the old people are surely abrogated and have ceased; and in their stead the symbols of the New Testament are placed – baptism in the place of circumcision, the Lord's Supper in place of the Paschal Lamb and sacrifices... In baptism the sign is the element of water, and that visible washing which is done by the minister; but the thing signified is regeneration and the cleansing from sins... Baptism once received continues for all of life, and is a perpetual sealing of our adoption... To be baptised in the name of Christ is to be enrolled, entered, and received into the covenant and family, and so into the inheritance of the sons of God; yes, and in this life to be called after the name of God; that is to say, to be called a son of God; to be cleansed also from the filthiness of sins, and to be granted the manifold grace of God, in order to lead a new and innocent life. Baptism, therefore, calls to mind and renews the great favour God has shown to the race of mortal men. For we are all born in the pollution of sin and are the children of wrath. But God, who is rich in mercy, freely cleanses us from our sins by the blood of his Son, and in him adopts us to be his sons, and by a holy covenant joins us to himself, and enriches us with various gifts, that we might live a new life. All these things are assured by baptism. For inwardly we are regenerated, purified, and renewed by God through the Holy Spirit and outwardly we receive the assurance of the greatest gifts in the water, by which also those great benefits are represented, and, as it were, set before our eyes to be beheld... And therefore we are baptised, that is, washed or sprinkled with visible water. For the water washes dirt away, and cools and refreshes hot and tired bodies. And the grace of God performs these things for souls, and does so invisibly or spiritually... We condemn the Anabaptists, who deny that newborn infants of the faithful are to be baptised. For according to evangelical teaching, of such is the kingdom of God, and they are in the covenant of God. Why, then, should the sign of God's covenant not be given to them? Why should those who belong to God and are in his Church not be initiated by holy baptism? We condemn also the Anabaptists in the rest of their peculiar doctrines which they hold contrary to the word of God. We therefore are not Anabaptists and have nothing in common with them.[9]

I make no comment on all that except to repeat what I said; namely, that I have answered all these claims elsewhere. I urge all my readers to cultivate the Berean spirit (Acts 17:11).

---

[9] Chapters X, XIX, XX.

# Two Phrases to be Reckoned With

In various works, written and spoken, I have set out the biblical arguments for the all-important covenant-discontinuity brought about by Christ when he fulfilled the old covenant and rendered it obsolete, bringing in the new to supersede it. Two biblical phrases encapsulate some of the most glorious aspects of this watershed of the ages. All I want to do in this very short article is list some of the ways Scripture uses these two phrases, to let them speak for themselves. My aforesaid works contain my justifying arguments for the many implications of these passages.

### Phrase 1: 'but now'

I restrict my selection to Paul's letter to the Romans.

> By works of the law no human being will be justified in [God's] sight, since through the law comes knowledge of sin. *But now* the righteousness of God has been manifested apart from the law, although the law and the prophets bear witness to it – the righteousness of God through faith in Jesus Christ for all who believe (Rom. 3:20-22).

> When you were slaves of sin, you were free in regard to righteousness. But what fruit were you getting at that time from the things of which you are now ashamed? For the end of those things is death. *But now* that you have been set free from sin and have become slaves of God, the fruit you get leads to sanctification and its end, eternal life (Rom. 6:20-22).

> While we were living in the flesh, our sinful passions, aroused by the law, were at work in our members to bear fruit for death. *But now* we are released from the law, having died to that which held us captive, so that we serve in the new way of the Spirit and not in the old way of the written code (Rom. 7:5-6).

> There is therefore *now* no condemnation for those who are in Christ Jesus. For the law of the Spirit of life has set you free in Christ Jesus from the law of sin and death. For God has done what the law, weakened by the flesh, could not do. By sending

his own Son in the likeness of sinful flesh and for sin, he
condemned sin in the flesh, in order that the righteous
requirement of the law might be fulfilled in us, who walk not
according to the flesh but according to the Spirit (Rom. 8:1-4).

Just as you were at one time disobedient to God *but now* have
received mercy because of their [that is, Israel's] disobedience,
so they too have *now* been disobedient in order that by the
mercy shown to you they also may *now* receive mercy. For
God has consigned all to disobedience, that he may have mercy
on all (Rom. 11:30-32).

Now to him who is able to strengthen you according to my
gospel and the preaching of Jesus Christ, according to the
revelation of the mystery that was kept secret for long ages *but
has now* been disclosed and through the prophetic writings has
been made known to all nations, according to the command of
the eternal God, to bring about the obedience of faith to the
only wise God be glory forevermore through Jesus Christ!
Amen (Rom. 16:25-27).

See also John 15:22,24; Acts 17:30; 1 Cor. 15:20; Gal. 4:9; Eph.
2:12-13; 5:8; Col. 1:26; Heb. 8:6; 9:26; 12:26; 1 Pet. 2:10.

It is the *eschatological*[1] 'but now' which is at the root of the
apostle's argument throughout Romans and elsewhere. Paul
speaks of the age from Adam to Moses – before the law; then
the age of Moses – the reign of the law; and then the age of
Christ by his Spirit – after the law, the reign of grace. Once
again, it is this towering view of salvation history, and, in
particular, the contrast between the age of the law, and the age
after the law, which is vital. Paul is here clearly contrasting the
realms of law and grace, the realms of the old age and the new,
both in history *and* in the believer's personal experience. Above
all, the latter – but securely based on the former. Without the
historical, eschatological 'but now', there would be no personal

---

[1] I am using 'eschatological' to speak of the way God deals with men
through changing history; supremely, the end of the old covenant, the
inauguration of the new leading to the eternal kingdom. See my
*Redemption History*.

'but now'. And without the personal 'but now', there is no salvation.

### Three testimonies:

D.Martyn Lloyd-Jones aptly entitled his opening chapter on Romans 3:21-22: 'The Great Turning Point – "But Now"'. As he said, it is these two words, 'but now', which are vital. 'What then is their meaning and import?' He answered his question:

> They do two main things. First and foremost they provide us with a contrast... to all the old law position, to our being under the law in any shape or form. But in addition to that, of course, the 'but now' brings in the time factor... What [Paul] is saying is, 'NOW' this thing that has happened [Christ has come, and so on] has changed everything.

Having rightly stressed the continuity between the law and the gospel – 'the law and the prophets witnessed to' the gospel – Lloyd-Jones then spoke of:

> What the position was under the law... but it is no longer like that. Something new has happened – 'now'. The great turning point in all history had just taken place: that was the coming of the Son of God into the world. So that we are living in a new age – the 'now'. It is no longer the old, it is the new age. It has arrived... This is a most important word to watch, therefore, as you read the New Testament; there is a contrast between what once was and what is now.[2]

As Douglas J.Moo put it:

> 'But now' marks the shift in Paul's focus from the old era of sin's domination to the new era of salvation. This contrast between two eras in salvation history is one of Paul's most basic theological conceptions... Romans 1:18 – 3:20 has sketched the spiritual state of those who belong to the old era: justly condemned, helpless in the power of sin, powerless to escape God's wrath. 'But now' God has intervened to inaugurate a new era, and all who respond in faith – not only

---

[2] D.Martyn Lloyd-Jones: *Romans: An Exposition of Chapters 3:20 – 4:25. Atonement and Justification*, The Banner of Truth Trust, London, 1971, pp23,28-29,34-38,40.

after the cross, but, as Romans 4 will show, before it also – will be transferred into it from the old era. No wonder Lloyd-Jones can exclaim: 'There are no more wonderful words in the whole of Scripture than just these two words "But now"'.[3]

Thomas R.Schreiner:

> In... Luke and Acts... the law should be interpreted in light of salvation history. Now that the new covenant has arrived in Jesus Christ, the law no longer occupies centre stage. The law must be interpreted in light of Jesus Christ and his coming. It was the will of God to keep the law during the old era of salvation history, but the law... is no longer normative now that Christ has come.[4]

## *Phrase 2: 'just as'*

The great motive for the believer's progressive sanctification is not, as John Calvin taught, and so many believe, the whip of the Mosaic law, the so-called moral law – which, naturally, must produce a sense of fear. No! Far from it! The believer has to obey Christ's law, and is enabled to walk in the Spirit 'just as' or 'even as' Christ walked.

> We were buried therefore with [Christ] by baptism into death, in order that, *just as Christ* was raised from the dead by the glory of the Father, we too might walk in newness of life (Rom. 6:4).

> Welcome one another *as Christ* has welcomed you, for the glory of God (Rom. 15:7).

> Be kind to one another, tenderhearted, forgiving one another, *as God in Christ* forgave you. Therefore be imitators of God, as beloved children. And walk in love, *as Christ* loved us and gave himself up for us, a fragrant offering and sacrifice to God (Eph. 4:32 – 5:2).

---

[3] Douglas J.Moo: *The Epistle to the Romans*, William B.Eerdmans Publishing Company, Grand Rapids, 1996, p221.

[4] Thomas R.Schreiner: *40 Questions About Christians and Biblical Law*, Kregel, Grand Rapids, 2010, p179.

Wives, submit to your own husbands, as to the Lord. For the husband is the head of the wife even as Christ is the head of the church, his body, and is himself its Saviour. Now as the church submits to Christ, so also wives should submit in everything to their husbands. Husbands, love your wives, *as Christ* loved the church and gave himself up for her (Eph. 5:22-25).

Put on then, as God's chosen ones, holy and beloved, compassionate hearts, kindness, humility, meekness, and patience, bearing with one another and, if one has a complaint against another, forgiving each other; *as the Lord* has forgiven you, so you also must forgive (Col. 3:12-13).

Since [or *As*] therefore *Christ* suffered in the flesh, arm yourselves with the same way of thinking, for whoever has suffered in the flesh has ceased from sin (1 Pet. 4:1).

## Closing questions

Does your view of the relationship between the old and new covenants take full account of all the truth which lies behind these two vital scriptural phrases?

Let me put it another way: Are you gripped by the glorious eschatological truth in these phrases, or are you confined by the statements issued by men nearly 400 years ago who produced a Confession in accordance with their pre-supposed theological system?

Or do you never even bother with these two phrases?

# National Anthem Verses

God has left us in no doubt:

> Consider your calling, brothers: not many of you were wise according to worldly standards, not many were powerful, not many were of noble birth. But God chose what is foolish in the world to shame the wise; God chose what is weak in the world to shame the strong; God chose what is low and despised in the world, even things that are not, to bring to nothing things that are, so that no human being might boast in the presence of God (1 Cor. 1:26-29).

Not many noble. Even so, this extract leaves open the possibility that some of noble birth might be converted. In that spirit, I have penned some verses to add to the British National Anthem for the coronation of Charles III on 6th May 2023.

> *God save our crownèd king,*
> *May he be born again.*
> *God save the king.*
> *May he to Jesus flee,*
> *Redeemed by blood to be,*
> *Thus from his sin set free.*
> *God save the king.*
>
> *God save our crownèd king,*
> *May he to Jesus cling.*
> *God save the king.*
> *May he the Spirit prove –*
> *God's word to know and love,*
> *And live to God above.*
> *God save the king.*
>
> *May he to Jesus bow,*
> *On Christ true praise bestow:*
> *To him alone.*
> *To Jesus glorious King,*
> *May we all worship bring,*
> *His praises ever sing*
> *To him alone.*

# A Tale of Two Coronations:
## Farcical & Real

In opening this article, I find myself penning similar words to the way I opened my article on the funeral of Queen Elizabeth II. Here we go again!

It's a good job it's 2023. If I'd been writing this five hundred years ago, my next (very temporary) address, I suspect, would have been the Tower[1] on my way to the block (if fortunate) or the scaffold.[2] But fortunately for me, Charles Windsor is no match for Henry Tudor in the tyranny stakes. Nevertheless, even in these more genteel days I am still breaking one of sternest of stern, but unwritten, commandments: 'You shall not rock the boat!' Or, to put it another way: above all things, be a wise monkey![3]

A bit of history. In 1521, Henry VIII wrote a book against Martin Luther, entitled *Defence of the Seven Sacraments*, following which, Pope Leo X bestowed upon him the title 'Defender of the Faith'. In 1530, Henry broke with the Pope, and four years later Parliament passed a bill which, while it maintained Roman Catholic doctrine in England, made Henry his own pope. He was so taken with the title 'Defender of the Faith', it had to be included in the pompous but unreal[4] blurb: 'Henry the Eighth by the Grace of God King of England, France

---

[1] The Tower of London.

[2] The block could be fairly quick. A proficient axeman would do the job in one blow. But it might be bungled. The scaffold, however, meant a very short time hanging by the noose, followed by public, crude surgery without anaesthetic – emasculation and disembowelling while still alive, cutting the body into four, and so on. Not a very pleasant way to begin – and end – the day.

[3] A Japanese maxim. 'See no evil, hear no evil, speak no evil'. In other words, turn a blind eye, look the other way, go along with the pretence, and, above all, don't blow the gaff.

[4] King of France in 1534? England had lost that throne in 1453.

and Ireland, Defender of the Faith and of the Church of England and also of Ireland in Earth the Supreme Head'.

In 1553, Queen Mary I restored the Pope as the Head of the Church.

In 1559, Queen Elizabeth I chose to become the Supreme Governor rather than the Supreme Head of the Church.

From 1st May 1876 until 22nd June 1948, British Sovereigns were also known as Emperors of India (the first was Empress Victoria).

On 6th May 2023, Charles III will be crowned and duly pronounced to be 'Charles the Third, by the Grace of God of the United Kingdom of Great Britain and Northern Ireland and of His other Realms and Territories King, Head of the Commonwealth, Defender of the Faith', the Supreme Governor of the Church of England.

Harriet Sherwood:

> [Charles is] perhaps more naturally high church, with a particular affinity for an interest in Eastern Orthodox Christianity. The new king has also shown great interest in non-Christian faiths, especially Islam and Judaism.
> In 1994, Charles triggered controversy when he said he would be defender of faith rather than Defender of the Faith, in a desire to reflect Britain's religious diversity. There were suggestions that the coronation oath might be altered.
> In 2015, he 'clarified his position' in an interview with BBC Radio 2, saying his views had been misinterpreted. He said: 'As I tried to describe, I mind about the inclusion of other people's faiths and their freedom to worship in this country. And it's always seemed to me that, while at the same time being Defender of the Faith, you can also be protector of faiths'.
> He pointed out that [his mother] the Queen had said her role was 'not to defend Anglicanism to the exclusion of other religions. Instead, the Church [of England] has a duty to protect the free practice of all faiths in this country. I think in that sense she was confirming what I was really trying to say – perhaps not very well – all those years ago'.

Now, as he ascends the throne almost three decades after that controversy, most people would agree that Charles should champion the right to religious belief and practice of all his subjects, not just that of the dwindling number of people in the pews of Anglican churches.[5]

\* \* \*

Let's get down to brass tacks. All this coronation rigmarole about the Monarch being anointed 'Defender of the Faith', 'Supreme Head' or 'Supreme Governor' of the Church of England, comes, not from 1521 and all that, but from the time of the Fathers who, acting directly contrary to biblical teaching, had gone back to the old, Mosaic covenant and imported several elements of that covenant (along with paganism) into the new covenant. Having gone that far, the Fathers, in cahoots with the Roman Emperors Constantine and Theodosius, then cobbled together the monstrosity of Christendom,[6] the union of Church and State into one Commonwealth. The coronation charade of 6th May 2023 is just the latest glaring example of the sort of showy fandangle this disastrous conglomeration has produced this past seventeen hundred years. It may be a spectacular show, yes, but, in the words of Isaac Watts, it is nothing more than 'an empty show'.[7]

The coronation itself is a blatant aping of the anointing of Solomon by Zadok the priest and Nathan the prophet. Now that old-covenant coronation shadowed a reality to come; this latest coronation, however, is nothing but a symbolic performance, a copy of that earlier shadow; it is, in truth, a showpiece pantomime. A splendid spectacle, lavish, gaudy, opulent, glittering, dazzling, it may be – indeed, it is – but from the so-called sacred building itself – 'the house of God' – to the glittering trappings on the so-called altar, from the multi-

---

[5] Harriet Sherwood: 'King Charles to be Defender of the Faith but also a defender of faiths' (*The Guardian*, 9th Sept. 2022).
[6] See my *The Pastor*; *Infant*; *Battle*; Appendix 2 'Christendom' in my *Relationship Evangelism Exposed*.
[7] Taken from Isaac Watts setting of Psalm 17.

coloured vestments of the so-called priests to the smearing of a drop or two of so-called sacred oil on the chest of a mere mortal, pronouncing him to be a virtual god, the spiritual Supreme Governor of millions, the entire pretence is nothing but a piece of religious-political theatre, a pretence that the State and the Church like to connive over. It is Christendom gone mad! Or, in truth, Christendom as it really is! From Hubert Parry's setting of Psalm 122: 'I was glad when they said unto me: "Let us go into the house of the Lord"' to George Frederic Handel's 'Zadok the Priest', and beyond, the old-covenant, embellished by a Greek Orthodox chant, governs everything.

Come back Hans Christian Andersen: we desperately need your little lad to point out the obvious.[8] Well, I say 'obvious', but Christendom, I fear, has so long been in the driving seat, only a tiny minority – an ever-diminishing, minority – can see the obvious. In lieu of Andersen's lad, I have penned this article.

Going back to the original, Solomon's coronation was from beginning to end symbolic, designedly so: it foreshadowed and represented the one true King – the Lord Jesus Christ – and his coronation, his reign, his rule. Scripture makes it absolutely clear that all the old-covenant symbols were ineffective shadows, mere pictures of a coming reality – whether tabernacle or temple, priesthood or sacrifice, altar or sabbath – all were shadows, but the reality, substance, fulfilment would be Christ himself:

> These [elements of the old covenant] are a shadow of the things to come, but the substance belongs to Christ (Col. 2:17).

> [The symbols of] the law... serve [as] a copy and shadow of the heavenly things (Heb. 8:4-5).

---

[8] In the folk tale: 'The Emperor Has No Clothes', two conmen persuade an emperor that they can clothe him in a magnificent suit that is invisible to the ignorant. Everybody goes along with the pretence – the emperor is, of course, naked – until a lad in his innocency points out what everybody knows, but nobody wants to admit – or dares to admit.

The law has but a shadow of the good things to come instead of the true form of these realities (Heb. 10:1).

As Christ himself declared at the start of his earthly ministry:

Do not think that I have come to abolish the law or the prophets; I have not come to abolish them but to fulfil them. For truly, I say to you, until heaven and earth pass away, not an iota, not a dot, will pass from the law until all is accomplished (Matt. 5:17-18).

Well, Christ has come. And Christ has fulfilled the old covenant and its shadows. Moreover, Christ has established the new covenant. And in fulfilling the old covenant, and setting up the new and thus accomplishing the everlasting realities, Christ has rendered the old covenant and all its symbols obsolete:

In speaking of a new covenant, [God by Christ] makes the first one obsolete. And what is becoming obsolete and growing old is ready to vanish away (Heb. 8:13).[9]

Charles III will be a crowned-king, yes, but he will be merely a constitutional king, and that of a faded nation; he will be acknowledged as Supreme Governor of the Anglican State-Church, yes; but all will be brought about by a ritual based on an old, obsolete covenant. But the real King, the only King, the only Head of the elect, is the Lord Jesus Christ. And only he.

As a consequence, the entire shebang conducted at Westminster on 6th May is, from start to finish, not only a pretence; it is a spiritually diabolical – I use the word advisedly – nonsense, bolstered by a Christendom State-Church.[10] It is nothing less than the latest episode in centuries of corruption. I can understand the unregenerate going along with it, but how any genuine believer can get involved with such a Church utterly defeats me. Some scriptural passages spring to mind.

---

[9] 'Ready to vanish away' means it was rendered obsolete. See my *Christ Is All*.

[10] See my *The Pastor*; See Appendix 2 'Christendom' in my *Relationship Evangelism Exposed*.

Paul's words to believers who were listening to false brothers who wanted to bring the law of Moses, the old covenant, into the new, apply directly to this latest fandangle, and the State Church which sanctions it. The apostle declared:

> I am astonished that you are so quickly deserting him who called you in the grace of Christ and are turning to a different gospel – not that there is another one, but there are some who trouble you and want to distort the gospel of Christ. But even if we or an angel from heaven should preach to you a gospel contrary to the one we preached to you, let him be accursed. As we have said before, so now I say again: If anyone is preaching to you a gospel contrary to the one you received, let him be accursed. For am I now seeking the approval of man, or of God? Or am I trying to please man? If I were still trying to please man, I would not be a servant of Christ (Gal. 1:6-10).

I wonder just how many distortions of the gospel are played out in Charles' coronation! If Paul were alive today, I know what sort of thing he would say about such a blatant exhibition performed by professing believers, all in the name of Christ:

> Yet because of false brothers secretly brought in – who slipped in to spy out our freedom that we have in Christ Jesus, so that they might bring us into slavery – to them we did not yield in submission even for a moment, so that the truth of the gospel might be preserved for you. And from those who seemed to be influential (what they were makes no difference to me; God shows no partiality) – those, I say, who seemed influential added nothing to me (Gal. 2:4-6).

As he commanded the Corinthian believers:

> Do not be unequally yoked with unbelievers. For what partnership has righteousness with lawlessness? Or what fellowship has light with darkness? What accord has Christ with Belial? Or what portion does a believer share with an unbeliever? What agreement has the temple of God with idols? For we are the temple of the living God; as God said: 'I will make my dwelling among them and walk among them, and I will be their God, and they shall be my people. Therefore go out from their midst, and be separate from them, says the Lord, and touch no unclean thing; then I will welcome you, and I will

be a father to you, and you shall be sons and daughters to me, says the Lord Almighty' (2 Cor. 6:14-18).

God has made the position unequivocal:

Come out of her [that is, Babylon], my people, lest you take part in her sins, lest you share in her plagues (Rev. 18:4).

In light of such black and white scriptures, how can any evangelical be tangled up in the Anglican system? Let's not beat about the bush. As I have said, we are talking about a State-Church founded on a system devised by the Fathers based on the old covenant adulterated with paganism. Moreover, this State Church holds to baptismal regeneration for infants, with a so-called Supreme Governor who is a mere man, one who is almost certainly not regenerate and can see virtually no meaningful difference between the gospel and Judaism, Islam, Hinduism, Buddhism or any Eastern religion (indeed, he might even prefer some of the latter to what's he actually ended up with!), a system which has supplanted Christ by human priests, and so on? If this is not a Babylonian farrago, what is?

C.H.Spurgeon spelled it out in his infamous 1864 sermon 'Baptismal Regeneration':

'But', I hear many good people exclaim, 'there are many good clergymen in the Church who do not believe in baptismal regeneration'. To this my answer is prompt. Why then do they belong to a Church which teaches that doctrine in the plainest terms? I am told that many in the Church of England preach against her own teaching. I know they do, and herein I rejoice in their enlightenment, but I question, gravely question, their morality. To take an oath that I sincerely assent and consent to a doctrine which I do not believe, would to my conscience appear little short of perjury, if not absolute downright perjury; but those who do so must be judged by their own Lord. For me to take money for defending what I do not believe, for me to take the money of a Church, and then to preach against what are most evidently its doctrines, I say for me to do this (I judge others as I would that they should judge me) for me, or for any other simple, honest man to do so, were an atrocity so great, that if I had perpetrated the deed, I should consider myself out of the pale of truthfulness, honesty, and common morality.[11]

And, for my purpose here, for 'baptismal regeneration' read 'acceptance of, and submission to, any man as the pretended Supreme Governor of the *ekklēsia*, and all the other trappings of the State Church'!

King Jesus is King Jesus still. He alone sits on the real throne, the throne of the universe; and, especially the throne of his *ekklēsia*. No man. No Archbishop. No Pope. Not even Charles III. Whatever the tradition! Whatever the flummery! Whatever the TV coverage! Whatever the viewing figures! Above all, of course, Christ is no cardboard Monarch! As everybody will find out:

> God... commands all people everywhere to repent, because he has fixed a day on which he will judge the world in righteousness by a man whom he has appointed; and of this he has given assurance to all by raising him from the dead (Acts 17:30-31).

And as we know:

> God has highly exalted [Christ] and bestowed on him the name that is above every name, so that at the name of Jesus every knee should bow, in heaven and on earth and under the earth, and every tongue confess that Jesus Christ is Lord, to the glory of God the Father (Phil. 2:9-11).

As John, in vision, saw:

> Then I saw heaven opened, and behold, a white horse! The one sitting on it is called Faithful and True, and in righteousness he judges and makes war. His eyes are like a flame of fire, and on his head are many diadems, and he has a name written that no one knows but himself. He is clothed in a robe dipped in blood, and the name by which he is called is The Word of God. And the armies of heaven, arrayed in fine linen, white and pure, were following him on white horses. From his mouth comes a sharp sword with which to strike down the nations, and he will rule them with a rod of iron. He will tread the winepress of the

---

[11] Spurgeon sermon 573.

fury of the wrath of God the Almighty. On his robe and on his thigh he has a name written, KING OF KINGS AND LORD OF LORDS (Rev. 19:11-16).[12]

Figurative language? Yes. But that figurative language bespeaks an aweful – literally, full of awe – reality. *Christ is the real KING.*

As the psalmist reminded all who are in authority, so I remind Charles and Camilla:

> You are gods [that is, princes, rulers], sons of the Most High [that is, by God's will, in high office], [both] of you; nevertheless, like men you shall die, and fall like any prince (Ps. 82:6-7).

And as the psalmist urged his readers, so I urge you, reader:

> Kiss the Son, lest he be angry, and you perish in the way, for his wrath is quickly kindled. Blessed are all who take refuge in him (Ps. 2:12).

---

[12] See my 'The Real King' on my sermonaudio.com webpage.

# An Appeal to the Reformed

I have a problem, a problem which only the Reformed can solve. I appeal to them to help me.

During years of engaging with the works of covenant theologians over the law, I have tried time and again to get them to think about Scripture unfettered by one or another of the Reformed Confessions.[1] But I always come up against the same brick wall. Whenever I read a work on the law – or some topic connected to the law – by a covenant theologian, I always meet the same three adjectives – moral, ceremonial and judicial, or their equivalents. It seems as though covenant theologians cannot think about, read or write the word 'law' without calling upon these three adjectives. Do they have a box of them to hand? It reminds me of somebody curling up on the settee on a Friday night, switching on the TV, and, from time to time, while their eyes are still glued to the screen, a skilful hand instinctively dips into a box of chocolates to select a favourite – Turkish Delight, Caramel, or Brazil Nut. When the programme gets exciting, threatening or whatever, pop another chocolate in the mouth and chew the faster.

But it isn't funny!

No, it is not!

Serious issues are involved; very serious. By imposing these three adjectives on Scripture, covenant theologians bolster their theological system, and so utterly fail to see the glorious biblical doctrine of the covenants. How ironical – the biggest mistake that covenant theologians make is their complete misunderstanding of the biblical doctrine of the covenants! And the consequences of this are far-reaching – far beyond the ivory

---

[1] Do they read Scripture without the Confession in mind? I've given up trying to get them *discuss* Scripture unfettered. See my 'Flogging a Dead Horse'.

tower of the minister's study. Because of it, the man, woman and young person in the pew – and in many cases, at the font – are loaded with immense problems and hurts. Unbelievers can be led through years of torture as they are prepared for Christ, prepared by repeated doses of the law to produce what many Reformed think of as 'a thorough law work'. Infants can – countless numbers do – grow up thinking that because a parent was 'in the covenant' and had them sprinkled as babies, they, too, are 'in the covenant', or somesuch jargon. Because of law-teaching, believers can spend many anxious years in lack of assurance, smarting under heavy lashes with the (to use John Calvin's word) whip of the law, being told again and again that the height of spirituality is to know and feel that you are 'the wretched man of Romans 7:14-25'. These consequences, and others like them, are the heavy pastoral fall-out of covenant theology. I don't engage with the Reformed over the law as some sort of a chess match, a battle of wits over texts. Think of it as the emergency ward of a hospital. Life and death issues – spiritual life and death issues – are at stake.

And, as I say, at the heart of this debate is this matter of the so-called threefold division of the law into moral, ceremonial and judicial. This invention is the lynchpin of covenant theology.

Now, as I have argued time and time again,[2] this so-called threefold division of the law is unscriptural. Probably dreamed up by Thomas Aquinas, set in concrete by John Calvin, it was adopted wholesale by the Puritans, and so dominated both the Westminster Confession of Faith and the 1689 Baptist Confession, and has exercised a widespread influence over evangelicals ever since, including men like C.H.Spurgeon and D.Martyn Lloyd-Jones.[3] For all that, I, along with many others, still assert that it is unscriptural.

Now... here's my problem. This is where we reach the nub of it. It is always hard to prove a negative. It can be done, but proof of

---

[2] See above all, my *Christ Is All*.
[3] Both men were contradictory over the law. See my *Spurgeon*; 'Lloyd-Jones for Law Men' in my *New-Covenant Articles Volume Four*.

a negative is never – to my mind – quite as convincing as proof of the positive. In any case, the burden of proof in this case lies with the Reformed. They assert that the law is divided into three; I, as just one among many, say it is not. The ball is in their court – they make the assertion; they should prove it.

Let me illustrate my point. All illustrations fail, but at least let me try.

First from the field of Mathematics. Pythagorean Triples exist. Take the integers 3,4,5. We know that $3^2 + 4^2 = 5^2$. The same goes for 5,12,13 and 7,24,25, and so on. But nobody has ever found three integers for the power three and above; that is, nobody has found three integers to satisfy $a^3 + b^3 = c^3$, and so on. Until recently, however, it had to be admitted that just because nobody – so far – had come up with such a set of integers, it did not mean that somebody, tomorrow, might not find a set. A million, million failures does not prove that it is impossible. Proving – proving, I repeat – the negative can be very difficult.[4] How much easier for those who say three such integers exist! Just produce them!

Take the legal system. Margaret Fleming was reported missing in 2016. She had not been seen by any independent witness since 1999. Her two carers had continued to claim her benefits over those years. In 2019, the carers were convicted of Margaret's murder. But the prosecution had a very difficult task: no body was found, no body could be produced. The defence could argue that though Margaret might have been missing for those years, she might walk in tomorrow. 'Beyond reasonable doubt' is essential for a conviction. Who could be certain that Margaret was dead? If she was dead, where was the body, where was the D.N.A proof, where was the link to the carers? Make no mistake: if the prosecution could have produced the body, it would have done so – like a shot! If forensics could have linked

---

[4] For those with a strong constitution, that very difficult proof in this case, may be found in Andrew John Wiles: 'Modular elliptic curves and Fermat's Last Theorem', *Annals of Mathematics*, 141,1995.

the carers to the corpse, the prosecution would have produced the evidence in court. Produce the body! Give us the proof!

The upshot? I can argue 'til the cows come home that Scripture never uses the threefold division, that Scripture never justifies such a division. But this still leaves the ball firmly in the Reformed court. Even so, it's a doddle for them! Just produce the proof, the evidence! They've had hundreds of years to come up with it.

Let me be clear. No quotation from Aquinas, Calvin, a score of Puritans, any Confession, Spurgeon, Lloyd-Jones or Uncle Tom Cobley is proof. Proof and justification must come from Scripture, and Scripture only.

So I appeal to the Reformed. You can put this issue beyond doubt once and for all. Produce the proof – that's all you have to do. Otherwise, admit the truth of what you are doing – which everybody knows you are doing – that you are breaking your own Confessions and making the inventions of men – and not Scripture – the authority for what you teach. Or... drop your use of the threefold division of the law.

By the way, Scripture does speak of a division in the matter – not the Reformed threefold division, of course, but a twofold division between law and grace. I restrict my extracts to where the contrast is explicit. Many more passages speak in similar terms, of course:

> The *law* was given through Moses; ***grace*** and truth came through Jesus Christ (John 1:17).

> For by works of the *law* no human being will be justified in his sight, since through the *law* comes knowledge of sin. But now the righteousness of God has been manifested apart from the *law*, although the *law* and the prophets bear witness to it – the righteousness of God through faith in Jesus Christ for all who believe. For there is no distinction: for all have sinned and fall short of the glory of God, and are justified by his ***grace*** as a gift, through the redemption that is in Christ Jesus (Rom. 3:20-24).

The *law* came in to increase the trespass, but where sin increased, *grace* abounded all the more (Rom. 5:20).

Sin will have no dominion over you, since you are not under *law* but under *grace* (Rom. 6:14).

I do not nullify the *grace* of God, for if righteousness were through the *law*, then Christ died for no purpose (Gal. 2:21).

You are severed from Christ, you who would be justified by the *law*; you have fallen away from *grace* (Gal. 5:4).

Now let's have a discussion on that basis, without any smokescreen of a so-called threefold division of the law!

Printed in Great Britain
by Amazon

32621390R00109